Developing the Individual

Tony Grundy and Laura Brown

- Fast-track route to a proactive, individually tailored approach to personal development as a long-term strategy with measurable payback

- Covers options for development including formal training and on-the-job learning, as well as diagnosing development needs, developing and evaluating options, and evaluating the return on development

- Case studies from The Dowty Group, Mercury Communications and Hewlett-Packard

- Includes a comprehensive resources guide, key concepts and thinkers including Chris Agyris and Peter Senge, a 10-step action plan for developing the individual, and a section of FAQs

TRAINING & DEVELOPMENT

11.09

>>EXPRESS EXEC.COM<<
essential management thinking at your fingertips

GW00501437

First Published 2003 by
Capstone Publishing Limited (a Wiley company)
8 Newtec Place
Magdalen Road
Oxford OX4 1RE
United Kingdom
http://www.capstoneideas.com

CIP catalogue records for this book are available from the British Library and the US Library of Congress

ISBN 1-84112-450-8

Printed and bound in Great Britain by T.J. International Ltd, Padstow, Cornwall

Wiley also publishes its books in a variety of electronic formats. Some content that appears in print may not be available in electronic books.

Websites often change their contents and addresses; details of sites listed in this book were accurate at the time of writing, but may change.

Contents

Introduction to ExpressExec

ExpressExec is a completely up-to-date resource of current business practice, accessible in a number of ways – anytime, anyplace, anywhere. ExpressExec combines best practice cases, key ideas, action points, glossaries, further reading, and resources.

Each module contains 10 individual titles that cover all the key aspects of global business practice. Written by leading experts in their field, the knowledge imparted provides executives with the tools and skills to increase their personal and business effectiveness, benefiting both employee and employer.

ExpressExec is available in a number of formats:

» **Print** – 120 titles available through retailers or printed on demand using any combination of the 1200 chapters available.
» **E-Books** – e-books can be individually downloaded from ExpressExec.com or online retailers onto PCs, handheld computers, and e-readers.
» **Online** – http://www.expressexec.wiley.com/ provides fully searchable access to the complete ExpressExec resource via the Internet – a cost-effective online tool to increase business expertise across a whole organization.

» **ExpressExec Performance Support Solution (EEPSS)** – a software solution that integrates ExpressExec content with interactive tools to provide organizations with a complete internal management development solution.

» **ExpressExec Rights and Syndication** – ExpressExec content can be licensed for translation or display within intranets or on Internet sites.

To find out more visit www.ExpressExec.com or contact elound@wiley-capstone.co.uk.

Introduction

» The context
» Strategies for developing the individual
» Value added by individual development
» Individual development and breakthrough theory
» Summary

THE CONTEXT

Even before the recession of the early 1990s, managers were becoming more alert to the need to take more control and to have more influence over their development. Previously, there was more emphasis on the individual's organization as the primary guardian of development.

For example, when one of the authors worked for the British oil company BP in the early 1980s, each new manager had a program of development laid out for them, in keeping with the organizational hierarchy as it was then. At that time, self-development was not on the radar map. For example, the very idea of deciding to put oneself on a master of business administration (MBA) course was almost unthinkable. One of the authors used to joke of the hierarchy: "By the time I get into a really senior position at BP and get a company car, I will probably have to drive a Reliant Robin."[1]

Since then, organizations and careers have changed and become far more uncertain, generating a surge of interest in individuals driving their own development. From the mid-1990s onwards, there has been a rapid increase in the growth of public courses (especially short courses, meaning that managers do not have to catch up on too much work when they go back). These changes have mixed benefits and costs; as we will argue in Chapter 7, successful individual development is often accompanied by organization-wide support for learning.

Although a broad range of developmental strategies for the individual exists – namely courses (such as MBAs), projects, secondments, coaching, and monitoring – the default solution is very often still the training course. In many ways this is a pity, because it is not always the case that training generates significant learning; such learning should produce a real change in capability and in action, thus developing the individual.

Indeed, the very notion that *everyday work* presents one of the best possible developmental activities seems to have gone by the board. Don't get us wrong, courses do have their own role to play. Especially at the start and in the early–middle phases of a career, it is useful to digest sufficient mental frameworks and maps to be able to deal with complex issues easily and quickly – and, above all, with confidence.

Table 1.1   Major benefits of courses taken by one of the authors.

Courses	Major benefits
First degree (behavioral sciences)	Analytical understanding
Chartered accountant	Strategic thinking *and* confidence
	Entry to strategy consultancy
MBA	Strategic thinking *and* confidence
	Entry to strategy consultancy
PhD (strategic management)	New frameworks/products
	Credibility as a strategy consultant
	Entry to business school lecturing
	Confidence as a writer
	Two books authored
MPhil (strategic management)	Greater strategy facilitation capability
	One book authored
MSc (organizational behavior)	Human resources strategy product

But everyday work is often the best opportunity for learning and development.

Looking back on the developmental path of one of the authors, it is not difficult to identify the major benefits of the courses that he did (Table 1.1). It is interesting at this point to reflect on the value (financially speaking) of this kind of development. Each one of these courses generated an incremental income stream.

This brings us to a number of key points.

» Developmental investment by the individual(s) can potentially produce a huge pay-off.
» Developmental activities need to form part of a longer-term strategy. Also, they typically add value through being part of a set, rather than making a relatively isolated contribution.
» This developmental strategy should be thought through as a series of stages or as a sequence of pre-orchestrated moves.

We now turn to strategies for developing the individual, and then go on to consider the value added by individual development.

STRATEGIES FOR DEVELOPING THE INDIVIDUAL

There are a number of strategies for developing the individual, some of which have already been touched upon. These include:

» on-the-job development;
» in-company training;
» public training programs;
» consortia programs;
» formal management education, including:
  » professional qualifications;
  » an MBA; or
  » an MSc in a specialist area such as corporate finance, human resources (HR) development, or strategic change;
» actually reading (and digesting) quality management books and articles;
» working on a real strategic change project;
» a group learning project;
» an individual learning project;
» benchmarking opportunities;
» shadowing someone in another industry;
» mentoring with a senior line manager;
» coaching, perhaps with a specialist, outside the company;
» a secondment within the company;
» a secondment outside the company; and
» a challenging short-term role, designed to develop a targeted number of competencies.

Each of the strategies needs to be evaluated for each and every individual. We will be going on to this at a more detailed level in Chapter 4. But, at a more generic level we can still characterize these strategies for individual development (Table 1.2). Ideally, the individual should pick from the most appropriate of these opportunities, depending upon their situation. For instance, if they are seeking exposure to other companies' thinking, then a public training program, an MBA, or a consortia program (if available) could be ideal.

Also, a professional qualification might be more appropriate at an earlier career stage. However, an MBA, an MSc, or a public

Table 1.2 An overview of strategies for developing the individual.

Training	Advantages	Disadvantages
On-the-job development	It has immediate benefits	Real-life experiment is perceived as too dangerous
In-company training	Highly relevant (hopefully) to the work we actually do	It doesn't (easily) bring in an external perspective
Public training programs	Mixing with people from other companies	This is typically low-reality learning
Development consortia	Gets the best of both worlds (in-company and public course training)	These are typically difficult to set up – and to sustain
Professional qualifications	Can give a tangible edge in terms of both role and rewards (depending upon the qualification)	Might well limit career opportunities (subsequently) to a specific type of role
MBA	A high status qualification	This might be pursued as an end-in-itself
	Salary premium	Not always as high as you might think
	Learning and increased capability	Lots and lots of time input
MSc	Signals a higher level of competence	Sometimes overly academic
	Quicker than an MBA (and less time input)	Might not have the status of an MBA

general management course would probably be more useful during the transition from early to mid-career.

We now turn to various forms of learning and development projects (Table 1.3). From these, we can see that the choice of project will depend upon the degree of stretch being sought, as well as the level of pre-existing self-confidence.

Next, we move on to developmental processes (Table 1.4). Shadowing entails spending a day or two with a manager in another industry. Mentoring is an internal process and works well if there is a close trust between the mentor and the manager, and if the mentor is highly

Table 1.3   An overview of learning and development projects.

Projects	Advantages	Disadvantages
Group learning projects	More learning in teams	More time-consuming and potentially difficult behaviorally/politically
Individual learning projects	Personal sense of stretch and achievement	Might be more difficult analytically
Real strategic change projects	Real business value added	Can get so real that learning disappears from the agenda
	Highly stretching developmentally	Might be a high risk career-wise

Table 1.4   An overview of developmental processes.

Processes	Advantages	Disadvantages
Shadowing someone in another industry	Very powerful and enlightening learning experience	Benefits might not be so obvious before the event
Mentoring within the company	Can be a great all-round and personalized development experience	Shortage of decent and appropriate mentors
Coaching, usually outside the company	Provides a sounding board from outside the company	Likely to be reasonably expensive

motivated to add value. Coaching (usually external) can integrate a whole variety of approaches such as personal/management style analysis, incorporating psychometrics; support in defining roles and tasks; problem-solving; prioritization; and strategic thinking.

Let us now look at developmental roles (Table 1.5). Once again there are many trade-offs to be made, but each one of these roles can

Table 1.5 An overview of developmental roles.

Roles	Advantages	Disadvantages
Secondment within the company	Broadens experience, without leaving the company	It may not be for long enough
Secondment outside the company	More scope to manage differently, and exposure to different ways of thinking	You might not wish to come back! (or experience re-entry problems)
A challenging short-term role	Excellent for developing specific target skills	Risk of failure in the role may be high, without support such as mentoring

accelerate learning, often much more effectively than formal training and related approaches.

It is also worth considering the developmental mix. Take the example of a high-flying accountant between the ages of 24 and 39 (Table 1.6). Notice how these training and other developmental activities are carefully sequenced and timed. For example, an MBA after age 35 might be a false move for this high-flyer.

VALUE ADDED BY INDIVIDUAL DEVELOPMENT

The value added by individual development occurs in a multitude of ways. First, to the individual, value can be added in a number of different ways, especially:

» better performance on the job, which in turn:
  » increases job satisfaction;
  » increases the probability of promotion;
  » brings forward the likelihood of promotion;
  » produces a solid track record as a solid basis for applying for better jobs in other (perhaps more attractive) organizations;
  » reduces stress; and
  » reduces time on the job;

Table 1.6 The developmental mix in the career of a high-flying young accountant.

Age	Training and development activities
24	Qualified as a chartered accountant
25	Management development course within the company (management and leadership skills)
26	Public programs in marketing and in IT strategy
27–8	MBA (part-time)
27	Secondment to a line position
28	Led a strategic change project
29	Promoted to business-level finance director
29	Mentored by a divisional chief executive officer
30	International assignment
32	Appointed divisional finance director within another group
32–3	MSc (part-time) in corporate finance
34	Secondment as group head of acquisitions and business development
35	Managing director of a significant operating unit
38	Promoted as group finance director
39	Coaching program (preparation for being group chief executive officer potentially)

» a higher salary and/or bonuses; and
» a sounder base for attracting further developmental opportunities (e.g. general management courses or an MBA).

The value added to the company can take other related forms:

» better performance in current roles;
» the creation of a bigger pool of strong executive talent (really excellent senior managers are still hard to find);
» the maintenance of employee satisfaction;
» a more open, challenging culture in the organization;
» better retention of key employees; and
» the attraction of high-caliber recruits (through a genuine commitment to investing in individual development).

Table 1.7 The career breakthroughs of one of the authors over the last decade.

Period	Career breakthroughs
1990–1992	Developing independent consulting skills
	Acquiring research skills (PhD)
	Writing first management book
1993–1994	Developing consultancy products/strategy skills
	Becoming a business school lecturer
1994–1995	Acquiring more all-round facilitation skills
	Becoming less of a workaholic
1998–2001	Skills for helping manage energy levels, both of himself and others
2002–2003	Developing skills in writing practical management guides
	Acquiring strategic coaching skills

INDIVIDUAL DEVELOPMENT AND BREAKTHROUGH THEORY

A *breakthrough* can be defined as "an initiative or action which produces a very major shift in performance or in capability – either at the organizational, developmental, team, or individual level." An interesting feature of breakthroughs is that they typically have to be relatively small in number to prove effective. In fact, breakthrough theory (or *hoshin* in Japanese) suggests that only between one to three breakthroughs can be pursued both simultaneously and effectively.

Let us look at the career breakthroughs of one of the authors over the last decade (Table 1.7). Notice that at times he focused on just one skills breakthrough and at other times on two or three, but never on four, five, six, or seven.

Then try to reflect on your own skills breakthroughs in the following exercise.

EXERCISE – IDENTIFYING YOUR SKILLS BREAKTHROUGHS (15 MINS)

1 What are the three skills breakthroughs that would advance you in relation to your next possible career move?

2 What are your options for achieving these breakthroughs?
3 What might the value be to you and your organization?
4 What might the business case look like for one or more of these?

SUMMARY

Flatter and changing organizations have meant that individual development is not just an add-on extra, but is an essential part of career development. Whilst the default developmental path is often one of formal training there are typically a wide variety of developmental options, which need to be tailored to the individual. Most managers and many HR professionals consider far too narrow a range of options here.

It is important therefore that the individual creates their own developmental mix, rather than getting sucked into the question of "What training should I ask for?" This learning and development should be focused primarily on a small number of learning and development breakthroughs (a maximum of three if success is to be had).

NOTES

1 The Reliant Robin was a three-wheeled economy car popular in the UK in the 1970s and the early 1980s.

Definition of Terms

INTRODUCTION

In this chapter, we run through some of the most important terms used in the field of individual development. These include:

» *training*
» *development*
» *learning*
» *the learning organization*
» *competencies*
» *gap analysis*
» *training needs analysis*.

TRAINING

Training can be defined as "a deliberate and programmed activity aimed at improving one or more specific skills, either off the job or on the job."

Training can either be a group or an individual activity, depending on the situation. The advantage of group training is that social interaction will:

» provide a stimulus to the individual to learn how to perform better;
» provide some performance benchmarks that will give feedback on whether performance has improved or not;
» facilitate the learning of tasks that have a social impact (which many have); and
» draw more energy and commitment from the trainee.

Training (even in groups) does not necessarily imply the existence of a trainer. The "deliberate and programmed activity" can be initiated purely by the trainee, or by a group of trainees who form part of a learning set (group-managing the activity).

An example of solo training is that of the Manchester United and England footballer David Beckham, who practices taking free kicks to perfection. Beckham's learning feedback loop does not involve a trainer – he is, in effect, for the most part his own coach.

Solo training is a most valuable way of developing, especially in an on-the-job situation. Unfortunately, because of the discipline and commitment this requires, many managers default instead to periodic group-based learning. The problem here is that off-the-job learning does not necessarily translate into superior skills on the job, as the learning transfer may be inefficient.

DEVELOPMENT

Development can be defined as "the process of transforming an individual or group from one level of capability to another."

Development is a slightly different concept from training as it is:

» more broad-based, covering not just one skill or a number of specific skills, but a more generic capability (like leadership);
» long-term in its focus (frequently more than a year and perhaps longer); and
» generally more concerned with acquiring new skills, or applying existing skills in new ways.

Development is perhaps best seen as a process that might be made up into a number of phases. For example, to develop an effective general manager might require six phases:

» induction into the company/industry (phase 1);
» a first supervisory role (phase 2);
» specialist functional management skills (phase 3);
» general management training, by means of formal education (phase 4);
» mentored transition to a first general management role (phase 5); and
» a move to an overseas company to acquire international experience (phase 6).

Within each of the above phases, one might typically find more specific training on perhaps five or more key competencies.

LEARNING

Learning can be defined as "a conscious or subconscious process of developing or adapting perspectives to make better sense of the world, and to ultimately become more effective."

Learning may thus occur at a conscious or subconscious level. Indeed, highly successful managers are typically excellent at subconscious learning. Moreover, learning is built into their everyday routines for doing virtually everything.

Learning is not merely about adding to one's stock of knowledge, but it is frequently about changing it. The more successful learners are able to re-examine beliefs and thought processes, and discard them where they are no longer appropriate or applicable. For instance, in phase 2 of the individual's development illustrated earlier (a first supervisory role), a successful belief would be: "I need to actually do things myself to make sure that things get done, when these have not been done by other people."

A first line supervisor cannot delegate everything – they need to provide a focus for action. But in phase 5 mentioned above (mentored transition to a first general management role), this hands-on style would not only be unproductive, but it could even be a disaster. A successful general manager usually needs to step back from the detail and provide overall direction, intervening only selectively in what their staff are doing. Such interventions should be more concerned with steering and motivating the staff, than with fussing over the detailed content of their actions. This point is put more directly by the proverb: "Why keep a dog and bark yourself?"

Learning itself is a concept that can be developed further. For instance, Chris Argyris, who is profiled in Chapter 8, distinguishes between single-loop (simple) learning and double-loop (more complex) learning.[1] *Single-loop learning* involves "improving what you are currently doing," whilst *double-loop learning* involves "doing things in a new way, or learning how to do entirely new things."

Another perspective is to distinguish between operational (simple) learning and strategic (more complex) learning. *Operational learning* consists of "learning to do an existing task better, or to apply an existing skill to a task," while *strategic learning* is "a process of exploring complex issues affecting organizations, teams, and individuals." (The latter involves reflecting and debating on the interrelationships between these issues, and setting them against the bigger picture.) A summary

Table 2.1   Operational versus strategic learning.

Operational learning	Strategic learning
Programmed and deductive	Open, creative, and intuitive
Clear boundaries and structures	Ambiguous and ill-structured
Assumptions are given	Surfacing and questioning of assumptions
Linear and predictable process	Fluid and interactive process
"Hard" outputs (detailed but determinate)	"Hard" and "soft" outputs (patterns and hard insights coming out)
Low uncertainty and fear	High uncertainty, fear, and defensiveness

of the differences between operational learning and strategic learning is given in Table 2.1 .

THE LEARNING ORGANIZATION

Much has been made of the learning organization but few organizations appear to have been able to take on this model successfully. A *learning organization* can be defined as "an organization that uses organizational, group, and individual learning to continually transform itself and to meet its ongoing challenges, both consciously and unconsciously."

In an ideal learning organization:

» learning and experimentation are prized highly;
» learning is explicitly seen as producing better performance, and is conspicuously invested in;
» action and learning are equally valued;
» mistakes are recognized as inevitabilities and as potential positives, rather than as evils;
» individuals and groups are actually encouraged to develop and to adapt; and
» rigid mindsets and structures are regarded as no-nos.

Unfortunately it is easier to paint an idealistic picture of the learning organization than it is to actually create and sustain it.

In reality there are three schools of management thinking on the learning organization:

1 the *prescriptive* school, which believes that organizations must learn in order to survive and thrive, and become learning organizations;
2 the *impossibility* school, which believes that attempts to spread learning throughout any complex organization will founder upon a number of obstacles, such as denial of error, avoidance of uncertainty and ambiguity, or pure business politics; and
3 the *pragmatic* school, which believes that although there are many barriers to learning, islands or pools of learning can be created within an organization. These islands need a lot of effort if learning is to be developed and sustained. However, with continual effort, learning routines become built in to "how we do things around here" and may ultimately reach a critical mass to form joined-up learning continents.

(Note: the authors subscribe to the pragmatic school.) Let us briefly explore each school in turn.

The prescriptive school

The prescriptive school has many proponents, including Peter Senge in the US and Bob Garratt in the UK. While Garratt's main focus is on how management development can help an organization to become a learning organization, Senge is more concerned with the total functioning of an organization as an interactive learning system.

Adherents like to see learning in terms of challenge or contention, notably Tom Peters in *Thriving on Chaos*[2] and Richard Pascale in *Managing on the Edge*[3]. While highlighting the need to foster learning throughout complex organizations, they leave the practitioner wondering, "How do I begin?" and "How difficult or impossible is this Herculean task?"

However, the problem with these prescriptive ideals is that managers may be unable or unwilling to lead by example in changing their style. Without appropriate support and without mobilization as teams of "open thinkers," individual action is very likely to be frustrated.

The impossibility school

The impossibility school, by contrast, suggests that complex forms of learning are highly unstable, and are very difficult to share and sustain within an organization. Argyris argues that most managers are comfortable with simpler forms of learning, where the task around which the learning centers is repeated essentially in the same form or the same loop (hence *single-loop learning*). However, managers are much less comfortable with more open and unpredictable learning.

But just because organizations are not the most natural homes for learners does not mean that they cannot become learning organizations. Companies that have sought to introduce learning processes into the heart of organizational life include the American beverage giant Coca-Cola, the British financial services group Prudential, and the British supermarket chain Tesco.

The pragmatic school

There is a strong argument for the pragmatic school, given that the existing culture and mindset of most organizations is focused on short-term performance delivery. This means that existing management agendas are very much focused on *doing* rather than *learning*. Hence, the idea of the *learning organization* can seem somewhat irrelevant, or more of a matter for HR than for management. Learning as a core part of the management process needs to be gradually integrated rather than seen as a separate and all-encompassing initiative.

COMPETENCIES

There is a very extensive literature on management competencies. Indeed, competencies can give rise to almost a new industry of effort, as they can demand considerable effort to define, diagnose, and evaluate. A *competency* can be defined as "an area of skill that adds value, either now or potentially, to the organization."

Thus, competencies are not just things that you can do well or not so well, but have a very direct relevance to the organization and the way it generates economic value. Whilst the idea is more specific than that of "skills," because of the ambiguity around this, one sometimes feels nostalgic for the rather easier-to-grasp notion of "skills," which once upon a time seemed to do the job. Tesco, for example, has avoided the term *competencies* and adopted *success factors* instead, thus making sure that they make sense to their primary users – the line managers.

Unfortunately, the word *competency* does seem to be rather technical and may suggest more complexity than is actually needed. This, in turn, might lead HR staff (or the line managers) to produce excessively elaborate competency frameworks, sometimes with as many as 50 key competencies.

Whilst it is absolutely true that many management roles are highly complex skill sets, it is nevertheless likely that perhaps 20% of these competencies are the areas where the biggest gaps exist. Of these areas, maybe 20% are of the greatest importance. This complexity can be dealt with by focusing on the resulting 4% of competencies where there are big gaps that are also the most important gaps. (This is to take the Pareto principle – that 20% of things by number in any given population usually represent 80% of what is really important – to its logical conclusion.)

The key thing with competency analysis is to ask the question "So what?" This question entails:

» looking for patterns in underlying weaknesses across a number of competencies;
» seeking out one area, or a very small number of areas, of major breakthrough that can add the most value; and
» anticipating which kind of training and development options might be most suitable in locating the major (and most important) competency gaps in the organization (e.g. in-company courses, mentoring, culture change initiatives, or changes in performance management and other developmental processes).

The following is a brief example of how a broad-ranging competency framework can be defined. Here we have limited ourselves to just 20 key competencies. Whilst only a number of competencies are emotional rather than cognitive in nature, these more conditional competencies can prove more decisive in sustaining senior performance. (Note: such competencies are sometimes described collectively as *emotional intelligence*.[4]) Good instances of emotional competencies are personal charisma, drive, and empathy.

An example of a general management competency framework

Strategic thinking

Key competencies include:

» strategic analysis;
» creativity; and
» strategic facilitation.

Leadership and change management

Key competencies include:

» visionary skills;
» personal charisma;
» leadership style;
» change management; and
» project management.

Commercial skills

Key competencies include:

» marketing skills and customer focus;
» financial planning;
» negotiating skills; and
» international vision.

Problem-solving skills

Key competencies include:

» problem diagnosis;
» data collection and analysis skills; and
» prioritization.

Personal and interpersonal skills

Key competencies include:

» drive;
» time management;

- » influencing;
- » communication; and
- » empathy.

GAP ANALYSIS

Gap analysis goes back in time to the beginning of corporate planning in the 1960s when Igor Ansoff first popularized the topic.[5] *Gap analysis* can be defined as "the difference between where you are now and where you need or want to be in terms of capability at some future time."

Gap analysis is inseparable from "understanding what business you are in" (see also Chapter 6).

The need for a particular competency will change over time, for example with the growing demand for strategic thinking. Ten years ago strategic thinking was hardly on the agenda of most organizations, let alone on that of individual managers (except a very small minority of potential high-flyers). But nowadays strategic thinking is increasingly recognized by individuals, HR developers, and senior line management as a crucial skill.

TRAINING NEEDS ANALYSIS

Training needs analysis is a rather posh way of saying "skills diagnosis." A *training needs analysis* can be defined as "a systematic process for diagnosing current and potential future competency groups, prioritizing them, and suggesting some possible training options and solutions."

Because the three words *training, needs*, and *analysis* become more technical-sounding when bundled together in this sequence, it might be thought that a training needs analysis is of necessity:

- » complex
- » time-consuming
- » difficult.

This is not necessarily the case. Again, if one operates according to the Pareto principle (see "Competencies" above) then much of the work entailed in training needs analysis can be focused relatively sharply.

Also, as was suggested earlier with reference to competency analysis, the most important thing is to look for the big "So what?" questions. This entails identifying lines of enquiry (in the style of being a detective) as to which area of competency might generate the biggest wins.

Training needs analyses are usually carried out via a mixture of interviews and questionnaires. Generally speaking, interviews coupled with a semi-structured questionnaire appear to be a more successful approach than just questionnaires, as the terms used on questionnaires will frequently require explanation.

SUMMARY

Learning and development terms are often somewhat abstract, and require a lot of demystifying. For example, *competencies* can be more usefully described as *success factors*. Over-elaborate diagnosis, like extensive training needs analysis, can become an end in itself.

Developing the individual should be a reasonably simple, tangible, and logical process. This should focus on gap analysis, in which the gap is divided into a number of competencies, and the individual defines where they are now and where they need or wish to be.

NOTES

1 Argyris, C. (1991) "Teaching smart people how to learn", *Harvard Business Review*, May–June.
2 Peters, T. (1987) *Thriving on Chaos*. Macmillan, London.
3 Pascale, R.T. (1990) *Managing on the Edge: How the smartest companies use conflict to stay ahead*. Simon & Schuster, New York.
4 Goleman, D. (1996) *Emotional Intelligence: Why it can matter more than IQ*. Bloomsbury Publishing, London.
5 Ansoff, I. (1965) *Corporate Strategy*. McGraw-Hill, New York.

Evolution

- » Introduction
- » From on-the-job training to training programs
- » From training programs to training interventions
- » From company-led development to individual-led development
- » From tactical to strategic development
- » Summary

INTRODUCTION

In this chapter we examine major shifts in the development mix:

» from on-the-job training to training programs;
» from training programs to training interventions;
» from company-led development to individual-led development; and
» from tactical to strategic development.

The evolution of individual development is represented as a timeline in the box below. Further information on the key concepts and thinkers mentioned in the timeline can be found in Chapter 8.

A TIMELINE SHOWING THE EVOLUTION OF INDIVIDUAL DEVELOPMENT

» **1960s**: MBAs prove very popular in the US, and business schools are founded in the UK and Europe.
» **1971**: David Kolb maps out the *learning cycle* for the first time. His model becomes the foundation of much learning theory and practice.
» **1978**: Malcolm Knowles highlights that adults learn in very different ways to children.
» **1980s**: A second tier of business schools are founded as a result.
» **1980**: Reg Revans puts forward *action learning* as a way of operationalizing learning at both the individual and small-group level.
» **1981**: Stuart and Binstead emphasize that individual learning is a form of social interaction that cannot be separated from the organizational context.
» **1982**: Peter Honey and Alan Mumford use Kolb's model of the learning cycle and Knowles' emphasis on adult learning to categorize the different styles of individual learning.
» **Late 1980s**: Workshops prove popular in the UK and Europe.
» **1990**: Peter Senge advances the theory of the *learning organization*, proposing that an organization that values learning is able to help both the individual and the organization to develop more effectively.

» **1990–1994**: The world economic slowdown puts a dampener on the application of the learning organization. Most companies focus on restructuring and business process re-engineering instead.
» **1991**: Chris Argyris refines his work on *double-loop learning* so that it is more accessible. He argues that complex learning of this kind can be used by individuals and teams to reframe problems, rather than to diagnose them in a linear fashion.
» **1990s**: There is a rapid expansion of part-time and distance-learning MBAs. The MBA becomes slightly less prestigious and carries a lower earnings premium than before.
» **1995–2000**: The global recovery spells an increase in budgets for both group and individual training. The market for public courses expands as individuals increasingly see development as essential if career opportunities are to be maintained in a highly uncertain world.
» **2001**: September 11 means that many training organizations catch cold.
» **2001–2002**: The global economic slowdown results in training budgets being reduced. Meanwhile, the demand for qualified MBAs slackens.

FROM ON-THE-JOB TRAINING TO TRAINING PROGRAMS

Much training is traditionally initiated on an on-the-job basis. This can take a variety of forms:

» setting objectives for future performance improvement;
» regular performance reviews (measured against these objectives and in relation to specific job tasks);
» annual performance reviews;
» on-the-job projects; and
» operating procedure guides.

We now deal with each of these in turn.

Setting objectives for future performance improvement

Setting objectives for future performance improvement is one of the most immediate and practical ways of developing the individual. This can be used to:

» set stretching performance goals (notionally aimed at shorter-term performance, but also for learning and development generally);
» prioritize the set objectives (a good rule of thumb is to choose *no more than three* stretching objectives to focus on within a period of six to nine months);
» help identify *how* the individual will teach these goals effectively; and
» identify the kind of support needed from the individual's boss and other key people.

Regular performance reviews

Regular performance reviews (which may be done monthly) can help an individual to:

» identify unexpected difficulties in performing tasks really well;
» resolve these difficulties;
» reprioritize the difficulties where necessary; and
» provide positive reinforcement of ongoing achievements.

For example, one of the authors had a senior management role as head of finance and planning at the British bioscience firm ICI International Seeds. This author had weekly meetings with the deputy divisional finance director of ICI Agrochemicals, another British bioscience business. These sessions continued over a six-month period, in which the author was seconded from KPMG Management Consultants.

In the course of these sessions they were able to sort out:

» acquisition integration issues concerning a recent £50mn acquisition in Belgium and a £30mn acquisition in the US;
» reporting issues (the author was effectively reporting to two bosses, making work focus difficult);
» major transfer pricing issues in UK operations, where there were disputes with other parts of ICI;

» smooth delivery of the three-year plan for ICI Seeds; and
» quarterly reporting of results (especially how to position certain areas of not-so-good performance).

Looking back, and given the author's limited competency base for this job, it was hard to imagine how such a difficult job was achieved. This role had entailed being involved in:

» his first senior line financial position;
» a major change of focus from his consultancy role;
» an industry he knew nothing about;
» acquisition management, which he knew next to nothing about; and
» cross-border as well as multicultural management.

Regular performance meetings like this with a helpful coach can produce not just superior performance, but also greatly accelerated development.

Annual performance reviews

Annual performance reviews should be a higher-level version of regular performance reviews. Differences might include:

» more emphasis on looking at patterns in performance blockages rather than at isolated problems (which should be covered in more regular reviews);
» more time spent on the individual's developmental options and strategies; and
» more focus on specific off-the-job training opportunities.

Obviously, as these reviews are often linked to salary rises and provide input to potential promotion, they are more sensitive in nature; if handled badly, they can cause sudden switches in career direction.

On-the-job projects

On-the-job projects are a much underutilized area of development for the individual. These can take the form of:

» market research;
» a quality management review;

» a restructuring;
» product development;
» an acquisition;
» business process re-engineering;
» an IT project; or
» a business plan.

With projects of this kind, it is important to set both business and learning objectives, otherwise the business imperative will be considered to crowd out the learning focus.

But the beauty of on-the-job projects is that to a very great extent they can be self-driven. This improves the individual's ability to *learn how to learn*, which is a higher order management competency normally associated with high-flyers. Learning to learn entails:

» being able to monitor your learning;
» being able to make it much more efficient (i.e. getting the learning with less effort); and
» being able to make it considerably more effective (i.e. getting more value out of the learning, subsequently).

Operating procedure guides

Mention the words *operating procedure guides* and you may well start to yawn. But where these guides are appropriately written, they can provide an excellent way of helping the individual to pick up the culture and routines of a new organization. Also, in the right hands, they can provide a living guide to "how to do things effectively around here."

Some operating guides are now used in organizations in an extensive and ongoing way, for example:

» guides to strategic thinking (especially at the British supermarket chain Tesco, the British financial services group Standard Life, and the American computer software corporation Microsoft);
» guides to project management (as used at Tesco on major projects since 1997); and
» HR consulting guides (as employed at the Royal Bank of Scotland).

Table 3.1 An overview of on-the-job training.

Advantages	Disadvantages
Has immediate application	Too much of a focus on performance can drive out learning
Tangible pay-off/payback	Usually has short-term focus
Performance improvements on everyone's agenda	Perceived as time-consuming by the developer's manager

Table 3.2 An overview of training programs.

Advantages	Disadvantages
More far-reaching scope	Can be too diffuse, and unrelated to specific action
Longer-term development	Longer-term, potentially dubious payback
Benefits from safe, socially based learning	Can be treated as management holidays

These guides are no longer paper artifacts but come in electronic format, effectively representing a simple form of computer-based training. They are useful aids to on-the-job training.

Whilst on-the-job training has a very valuable and often overlooked role in development, it does need to be complemented by training programs. Some of the advantages and disadvantages of both forms of training are listed in Tables 3.1 and 3.2.

FROM TRAINING PROGRAMS TO TRAINING INTERVENTIONS

A training program typically takes the form of a short course – perhaps of one, two, or even three days' duration – involving:

» pre-work;
» goals and objectives;
» conceptual and practical input;

» practical group exercises;
» feedback sessions;
» distillation of learning lessons at group and individual level;
» action plans;
» handouts and checklists; and
» feedback (or "happy") forms.

Training programs are usually relatively self-contained. Attendees are rarely met individually or interviewed by training deliverers (unless a full training needs analysis is undertaken).

Whilst their overall skills gap may be known broadly, it is often not known in detail by individuals. Also training deliverers (especially external ones) may not have detailed knowledge of participants' agendas and mindsets ("Are they up for it, or not?") This makes it harder to ensure that the training is well directed and steered towards its real targets.

Hence, it is probably a "no-brainer" that training programs should:

» make a much greater effort with pre-work and follow-on work, *even if this requires more effort from HR* (a suggestion here is for HR to run fewer and higher-quality training courses instead of just "putting bums on seats");
» be positioned as an integral part of future management process and of "how we do things around here," rather than as a welcome break from normal work; and
» do a more thorough appraisal of training needs.

When these measures are put in place, we can begin to see the training program as more of a training intervention. The key differences between the two are shown in Table 3.3. Thus, a training intervention is very much a different beast to a training program. An excellent example of a far-reaching training intervention is that of Mercury Communications, the telecommunications subsidiary profiled in Chapter 7. This intervention had:

» very clear business goals;
» a number of phases (there was a series of interventions over a period of about four months);

Table 3.3 Training programs versus training interventions.

Training programs	Training interventions
Relatively stand-alone	A series of workshops/other interventions
A quick-and-dirty training needs assessment	A fuller training needs analysis is conducted
Narrow objectives (to deal with a specific symptom/problem)	Integrated with organizational goals/other interventions
Little reinforcement of learning or behavioral change	Considerable reinforcement of these shifts
Positioned by HR	Positioned by senior line management
Lower-reality exercises	High-reality work on major operational/organizational issues
Outputs presented to senior management as "interesting things to think about – and maybe forget"	Management actions and decisions actually change as a result

» positioning by the general manager, and active involvement through-out;
» real and tangible improvements to performance as a result; and
» major shifts in the capability of middle managers.

FROM COMPANY-LED DEVELOPMENT TO INDIVIDUAL-LED DEVELOPMENT

Whilst a high percentage of development is still organized for groups within an organization (as training programs/interventions), there is an increasing focus on individual-led development. This is partly as a result of a greater focus on empowerment (or enabling the individual to take more responsibility and control over their roles and careers in general). Also, individuals are increasingly eager for this following the massive restructurings and redundancies of the 1990s and the early 2000s (especially in the high-tech sector).

The contrasting philosophies of company-led development and individual-led development are summarized in Table 3.4.

Table 3.4 Company-led development versus individual-led development.

Developmental issues	Company-led development	Individual-led development
Developmental plans	Done mainly by the company	Done mainly by the individual (with their boss)
Training resources	Controlled by the company	Controlled at least in part by the individual
Training programs	In-company programs mainly	More public courses, or MBAs
	Delivered mainly through training courses	A wider variety of intervention (e.g. mentoring or coaching)
Career pattern	Assumed to be within the company	Portable capabilities/career

FROM TACTICAL TO STRATEGIC DEVELOPMENT

Tactical development aims to achieve performance shifts within three to six months. By contrast, strategic development aims to achieve performance skills over a period of three to eighteen months, and capability skills within a time horizon of one to six years. Tactical development is also more typically focused on narrower, relatively stand-alone objectives, whilst strategic development tends to have a broader range of objectives and to be interdependent with other initiatives, support processes, and interventions.

Narrower objectives are often associated with:

» technical training;
» presentation skills;
» influencing skills;
» supervisory skills; and
» functional skills.

Wider-ranging objectives might include:

» facilitating organizational change;
» making people more innovative;

» introducing project management processes;
» team-building;
» improving communication;
» strategic thinking; and
» commercial awareness and skills.

The latter objectives will typically require more time to deliver their full economic value. Also, they are more likely to require a training intervention than a discrete training program. In addition, they are more apt to have tangible business goals, as well as learning and development goals. They are also more liable to need a high level of consultancy diagnostic skills within HR, rather than a training needs analysis focusing on *the need as defined by management*.

Consultancy skills require more contact with line managers, deeper knowledge of their business and organizational issues, and a lot more time investment. (The latter is a big problem for HR staff who are still expected to do operational personnel roles, meaning that they are continually dragged into HR firefighting.)

ROYAL BANK OF SCOTLAND

Around 2000, the Royal Bank of Scotland, which had recently bought the British bank NatWest, decided to enhance the consulting skills of all its key HR managers.

The "consulting diagnostics" module within this program consisted of:

» the question "What is strategy/HR strategy?"
» understanding business performance – performance drivers;
» HR strategy in acquisitions – case study of BMW and Rover, the German and British car manufacturers;
» creating and evaluating strategic options;
» HR strategy in corporate turnaround/post acquisition – case study of the British health and fitness organization Champneys;
» diagnostic work on an HR issue;
» option generation – own HR issues;

» implementation analysis – own HR issues;
» stakeholder analysis – own HR issues; and
» uncertainty analysis – own HR issues.

This module is now supported by the Royal Bank of Scotland's HR consulting diagnostics tool kit.

Companies vary considerably in their degree of sophistication in this development area. There is a lot to learn by networking/benchmarking approaches, both with other companies and industries.

SUMMARY

Developing the individual has resulted in a number of major shifts in the development mix. Stand-alone, in-company programs are now managed more frequently as training interventions, and of a strategic rather than a tactical type.

Also, at a micro-level there is more of a role for individual-led development, manifested in the growth of short public courses, so that individuals can mix with staff from other companies and other industries.

With the spread of mentoring and coaching, the distinction between on-the-job and off-the-job training has become more blurred.

In Practice

INTRODUCTION

In this chapter we look at:

» diagnosing developmental needs;
» evaluating developmental strategies; and
» evaluating the return on development.

DIAGNOSING DEVELOPMENTAL NEEDS

There are three major techniques for diagnosing developmental needs. These are:

1 fishbone analysis – for understanding current skills gaps;
2 wishbone analysis – for creating a vision of the future; and
3 from-to analysis – for defining the key shifts in skills that are needed.

Fishbone analysis

Fishbone analysis is a useful pictorial technique for diagnosing skills gaps. The symptom of the skills gap is plotted to the right (as the fish's head), and the underlying causes of this problem are shown to the left as two columns of parallel lines that intersect diagonally (in a *fishbone* pattern).

By representing a case pictorially, it becomes much easier to:

» separate out the symptom from the root causes;
» mentally plot a large number of root causes;
» understand any underlying pattern in these root causes; and
» judge to what extent a training/development intervention can actively shift a particular case.

Figure 4.1 gives us an example of a rather spectacular diagnosis, performed by the authors on a manager who appeared in the ITV series *The Complainers* in the mid-1990s.

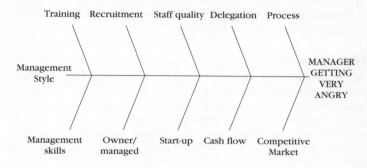

Fig. 4.1   Fishbone analysis of manager getting very angry.

THE COMPLAINERS – THE MANAGER BEHAVING BADLY

In *The Complainers*, an entrepreneurial manager is depicted in daily activity supervising his staff. There have been some rather major errors in the business, which places advertisements for companies. In this real-life documentary, the manager is very angry at the start, and becomes steadily angrier as his staff appear to wilt under the pressure of his criticisms. He increasingly loses the plot and eventually lifts the office table in the air, propelling it in the general direction of one of his employees who has just been fired.

(Note: Most viewers of this case want to see the action replay.)

Figure 4.1 suggests that the underlying causes of the manager's extreme behavior are to be found in:

» his management skills (perhaps he has had little or no management skills training?);
» his role in the business (which appears to be too dominant);
» his self-management capability (he appears to be unable to manage his frustration, going red at the beginning and turning a radiant purple towards the end); and

» his organizational skills (in terms of project management, delegation, coaching, interpersonal skills, etc.).

Wishbone analysis

Wishbone analysis is a helpful pictorial technique for creating a vision of future development. The vision is plotted to the left, and all the alignment factors are shown to the right as two columns of parallel lines intersecting diagonally (or so many *wishbones*). These are the necessary and sufficient conditions of creating – and sustaining – the vision.

Figure 4.2 illustrates an entrepreneurial manager with a vision to turn around his style to such an extent that he can win the Manager of the Year Award. In order to deliver and sustain this vision, the alignment factors might be to:

» go on the entrepreneurs' program at the Cranfield School of Management, south central England;
» undergo an intensive program of management coaching;
» take Valium for six months (without getting hooked);

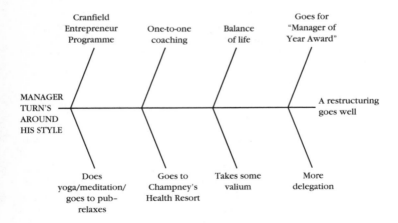

Fig. 4.2 Wishbone analysis of the turnaround manager.

» get a more balanced life;
» restructure his organization;
» delegate more;
» take up yoga and meditation; and
» attend the British health and fitness club Champneys once a month (if they will have him).

Obviously, when dealing with an individual who is in a turnaround situation, there may be a very real issue as to whether the alignment factors will *ever be in alignment*. We will leave the reader to judge whether a turnaround is actually viable in this particular case.

From-to analysis

One final stage is to look at what shifts are necessary to move from present to future capability. Essentially from-to (FT) analysis is an extended form of gap analysis, which can be used at individual, team, departmental, and business level.

Table 4.1 illustrates the key shifts in skills for our turnaround manager. The scores of 1 to 5 represent different levels of skill, depending on:

» where you are now (please be realistic!);
» where you actually need to be (not necessarily a 5);
» where the benchmarks, or your competitors, are; and
» what the most/least important skills are.

Table 4.1 From-to analysis of the turnaround manager.

From	Levels of skill					To
	1	2	3	4	5	
Very stressed						Very calm
Very frustrated						Very happy
Work is everything						Balance of life
Very sarcastic						Light humor
Over-controlling						Good delegation

EXERCISE – USING FISHBONE, WISHBONE, AND FROM-TO ANALYSIS (30 MINS)

For a developmental need in your business or in an individual, answer the following.

1 What is the major symptom of the skills gap? What are its root causes? (Try using fishbone analysis.)
2 What is your vision of future development? What alignment factors are needed to deliver it? (Try using wishbone analysis.)
3 What are the key shifts in skills for such development to be achieved? (Try using from-to analysis.)

EVALUATING DEVELOPMENTAL STRATEGIES

Developmental strategies have already been covered in Chapter 1. These included:

» individual training;
» group training;
» coaching and mentoring;
» on-the-job development;
» secondments;
» project work; and
» MBAs.

More interesting at this juncture is the imperative to evaluate the various developmental strategies formally. For this purpose we turn to attractiveness and implementation difficulty (AID) analysis, as demonstrated in Fig. 4.3 . This distinguishes between attractiveness (benefits less costs) and the level of implementation difficulty.

Figure 4.3 looks at the various strategies for developing our turnaround manager, such as:

» the Cranfield program (very attractive, but also very difficult – will our manager mix well?);

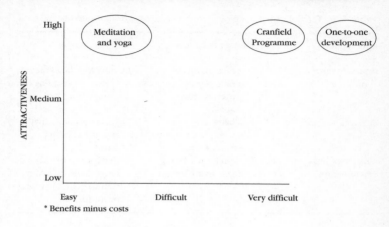

Fig. 4.3   AID analysis of the turnaround manager.

» one-to-one development (again very attractive, but somewhere between difficult and mission impossible – off the right of the graph); and

» meditation and yoga (who knows, these might have remarkable results – being very attractive and very easy – especially if our manager experiences health difficulties, which lead him to relax more).

AID analysis is invaluable for prioritizing all developmental strategies, as long as you bear in mind that:

1 implementation difficulty is invariably greater than you actually think; and
2 this difficulty is not just the initial implementation difficulty, but the cumulative sum of difficulty in achieving the desired result.

EVALUATING THE RETURN ON DEVELOPMENT

Development is frequently seen as being of intangible value, and inherently difficult to quantify in terms of tangible, economic, and financial benefits. However, this presupposition can be questioned;

Table 4.2 Tangible and intangible benefits of being a turnaround manager.

Intervention	Intangible benefit	Tangible benefit
Cranfield entrepreneurs' program	Understanding the difficulties of being an entrepreneurial manager	Eliminating the climate of fear, so avoiding major errors
One-to-one coaching	Realizing that you haven't got a strategy for something	Getting a strategy that avoids expensive errors
Balance of life (yoga and meditation)	Feeling better, being nicer, living longer	Earning more money for longer, and enabling staff to generate more profit for you

ultimately, it is very hard to think of anything of intangible value that is not also of tangible value, even if this does depend on contingent events.

Both the tangible and intangible benefits of turning around our entrepreneurial manager are listed in Table 4.2. In the end, every intangible goal can be cashed in by making it a tangible one. One should always remember that the ultimate value and cost drivers in any business are behavioral in nature, so development at all levels gives real competitive and financial advantage.

SUMMARY

Individual, and indeed organizational, needs are best diagnosed in the first instance through fishbone analysis. Once this diagnosis is complete, it is necessary to become more visionary using wishbone analysis, which requires a number of internal and external factors to be aligned. Thereafter, from-to analysis provides a better view of the developmental gap – and how it can be breached.

Developmental strategies can then be prioritized using AID analysis. Finally, by quantifying the intangibles, a start can be made on building an effective business case for development.

The Global Dimension

INTRODUCTION

In this chapter we look at the nature of:

» global management skills and careers;
» developing a global career; and
» developing a global organization.

GLOBAL MANAGEMENT SKILLS AND CAREERS

Global is an often-used, and perhaps much-abused, term in management. Here, *global* means "the management of strategies, markets, operations, and organizations across national borders."

So how do local and global management skills differ? Table 5.1 lists some of the key differences. These indicate that being an effective global manager requires the management of quite a number of additional perspectives and areas of complexity.

To diagnose your own skills as a global manager, we recommend that you do the exercise below.

Table 5.1 Local versus global management skills.

Local management skills	Global management skills
Focus on local markets, competition, and operations	Focus on a range of natural markets, competitors, and operational facilities
Locally based operations	Global centers of excellence
Local performance standards	World-class standards
Rooted in local culture	Worldwide customers
Divisional structures with simple reporting levels	Matrix structures with complex reporting lines
Managing upwards and downwards in the directory organization	Management of cultural differences
Local budgeting, planning, and financing	Global budgeting
Local finance operations	Global financial strategy
Local careers	Global careers

EXERCISE – ARE YOU A GLOBAL MANAGER? (15 MINS)

Using a scale of 1 to 5 (in which 1 = weak, 2 = moderate, 3 = average, 4 = strong, and 5 = very strong), try and rate the following of your global skills (Table 5.2).

Table 5.2   How do you rate your global skills?

Global skills	Weak	Moderate	Average	Strong	V. strong
	1	2	3	4	5
Experience of working in another country					
Globally based career ambitions					
Global knowledge of your function					
Global market/regulatory awareness					
Global awareness of competition					
Working with global customers					
Global awareness of operations					
Cross-cultural working/awareness					
Global business planning/strategy development					
Global acquisitions					
Global alliances					
Managing global restructuring					

(*continued overleaf*)

Table 5.2 (*continued*)

Global skills	Weak	Moderate	Average	Strong	V. strong
Project management across businesses					
Global influencing					
Global team management					
Foreign languages (general)					
Foreign languages (business)					
World-class benchmarking					
Global financial management and control					
Working across cultures					

Scores

80–100: Fantastic! Talk to the international headhunters now.
60–80: You are excellent material for an international career.
40–60: Work on your gaps.
20–40: You are local, not global, but why not consider global too?

DEVELOPING A GLOBAL CAREER

Specific ways of improving your global management skills and career
include:

» a posting to another country;
» a secondment to an international company or an overseas subsidiary;
» a project in another country;
» a course in international/global management;

» an international MBA, or an MBA with specialism in international management;
» world-class benchmarking;
» a global acquisition, alliance, or other business development; and
» joining another international company.

Let us now expand on each of these global career opportunities.

» A posting to another country is probably the most direct and rapid way of developing your international skills. A potential disadvantage is that you may get forgotten by your local HQ and find that the quality of any job on return is not so great, as you won't be able to network quite so well with domestic contacts while abroad.
» A secondment to an international company or an overseas subsidiary has the advantage of offering accelerated development as well as a ready return route. A disadvantage is that your personal life may be disrupted, as you probably won't be able to uproot all of your belongings (or even necessarily your family).
» A project in another country is another excellent route to acquiring global skills, without having the full disruption of an international move. However, it will probably demand a lot of time-consuming and exhausting international travel.
» A course in international/global management offers good low-reality learning and the chance to mingle with managers from other countries and industries. But, it may be short in practical application and will also be quite expensive.
» An international MBA, or an MBA with specialism in international management, opens up a career in a multinational/transnational company, gives you a global perspective on national markets, exposes you to world-class management practices, and is prestigious even for a locally based job. However, the teaching of your MBA may vary in quality from one business school to another.
» World-class benchmarking can be highly insightful, but only into one particular cut of global management – the specific object of the benchmarking.
» A global acquisition, alliance, or other business development provides a great opportunity to "have it both ways" – whilst you retain your base locally, you can get many insights into cross-border management

and strategy. The downside is that it often amplifies the risks already inherent in corporate development, particularly due to cultural differences across national boundaries.

» Joining another international company is a great idea, but it may be difficult to enter a senior role if you mainly have local experience.

The choice of a global career route can be made according to some quite clear questions, as you will see in the next exercise.

EXERCISE – A GLOBAL CAREER OPPORTUNITY OF YOUR CHOICE (15 MINS)

First, choose a global career opportunity, using the ideas above to help you. Then, try and decide how good a choice this would be in terms of the questions listed in Table 5.3, ranking the choice on a scale of 1 to 5 (in which 1 = poor, 2 = moderate, 3 = average, 4 = good, and 5 = very good).

Table 5.3   How do you rank the global career opportunity of your choice?

Criteria/questions	Poor	Moderate	Average	Good	V. good
	1	2	3	4	5
Strategic attractiveness					
Does this fit my personal values?					
Does it fit my personal goals and ambitions?					
Financial attractiveness					
What salary premium is available?					
Is the standard of living favorable?					

Table 5.3 (*continued*)

Criteria/questions	Poor	Moderate	Average	Good	V. good
Implementation difficulty					
How easy will I find the job to do?					
How easy will a return to my own country be?					
Uncertainty and risk					
Will the country be pleasant to live in?					
Will I have sufficient social support/friends?					
Acceptability to stakeholders					
Will my family/partner benefit significantly?					
Will they actually be losing out?					

(Note: the strategic options grid in Chapter 6 is another way of performing this kind of comparison.)

Scores

80–100: A fabulous move!
60–80: Probably a good idea.
40–60: Think very hard about it.
20–40: Don't do it!

DEVELOPING THE GLOBAL ORGANIZATION

Organizational development is difficult to achieve at a national level, let alone globally. Few organizations seem to have been genuinely successful in globally based interventions to develop capability. Exceptions might include:

» the British oil company BP (now BP Amoco), who brought about a culture change within the company;
» the British chemical company ICI, who shifted from using mainly British-born managers at senior level to using managers from all over the world;
» the British supermarket chain Tesco, who developed international retailing skills in addition to their existing domestic skills; and
» the American beverage giant Coco-Cola, who became an international learning organization.

Organizational development interventions at a global level require very active sponsorship by top line managers, astute HR developers with excellent facilitation skills, and occasional input by consultants. But when they do work well, they can generate some very real business benefits as well as capability benefits, right down to the level of the individual.

BEST PRACTICE – GLOBAL CULTURE CHANGE AT BP

In 1990, Bob Horton, the then chairman of BP (British Petroleum) initiated an unprecedented move to make BP world-class rather than parochial and bureaucratic. (When one of the authors worked for BP in the early 1980s, the joke in head office during the long, boozy lunch breaks was that "BP means 'Boring Petroleum.'")

By 1990, it was quite clear that this situation was no longer sustainable. BP was finding it increasingly difficult to retain its young high-potential managers. Worse still, in head office, decision-making was very ponderous, political, and difficult. The BP organization prior to that time might be likened to a super-tanker – which could *only just* change course, even if it spotted distant ships (or even icebergs) on the horizon. A more incisive simile might be that of a luxury liner on remote control – where the managers were able to hold 24-hour parties, without realizing that the liner was gently heading for the rocks.

The culture change initiative Project 1990 was launched by Bob Horton and, combined with major de-layering and re-engineering of BP's centralized structure, it cleared the way for a more open style of management.

For the individual, this offered a whole host of developmental opportunities, including:

» more upward career opportunities;
» more horizontal career opportunities (and in other countries);
» a personalized process for self-driven development and career-pathing;
» more projects, secondments, and opportunities for being monitored in the more open culture;
» much-improved training courses;
» more focus on benchmarking and on internal networking (for performance improvement, learning, and development); and
» more international postings (these were no longer as potentially disadvantageous now that there was less focus on head office careers).

From the individual's perspective, the bottom line of developing an organization is that more career choices need to reflect not merely the financial benefits and the status of joining a particular company, but also:

» its current global opportunities; and
» its future global opportunities.

SUMMARY

Global careers require a global management skill set, which has an expanded range of skills including matrix management, and competence in global management processes. There are many ways of gaining this experience, from project work in other countries to embarking on a career with a multinational.

Beware of joining a multinational that does not readily offer a global career because of its structure or politics. Also, avoid companies that offer one-way tickets to work in exotic places from which you might find it difficult to return.

The State of The Art

INTRODUCTION

Effective individual development involves using strategic learning to evolve your capability to a higher level. This is illustrated in Fig. 6.1.

Figure 6.1 begins with understanding your current position. This involves identifying both your *enabling advantages* (e.g. your core functional skills) and your *distinctive advantages* (e.g. your political skills or vision), as well as your personal *competitive disadvantages* (e.g. your poor time management or failure to think things through). It then explores what your career strategy might be. Depending upon the point you have already reached in your career and aspirations, your career strategy might have a timescale of three to five years, or possibly even longer.

WHAT BUSINESS ARE YOU IN?

When defining your organizational role, it is rarely self-evident "what business you are in." Although many roles are relatively fluid, it is still necessary to have a clear understanding of what is (or should be) at the core of this role.

The traditional way of defining roles in terms of your key fixed responsibilities is less relevant in an environment of continual change,

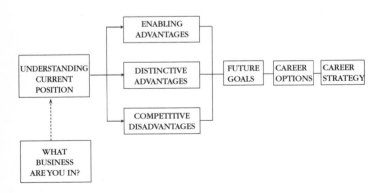

Fig. 6.1 Strategic learning and individual development.

which most managers now find themselves facing. Nevertheless, even in a fluid environment it is essential to understand how you currently *add value* to the organization and how you could *add more*. This added-value test is extremely useful, as it reinforces activities that you should be doing and questions activities of a less valuable or more dubious nature.

For instance, in an ideal world, a financial director might add value by:

» providing input to the strategic decision-making process;
» suggesting new areas for business development;
» keeping track of financial performance;
» interpreting this performance so that operational managers can take rapid corrective action;
» providing internal and external confidence in the business;
» satisfying regulatory requirements so that the business can continue to trade;
» optimizing the development of the company's financial resources, both long- and short-term;
» promoting a cost-aware culture;
» helping avoid both strategic and tactical blunders; and
» developing staff so that they understand the business and its finances.

Some of the above elements will not appear to be particularly new. However, some finance directors may place much emphasis on some areas, but less on others. For instance, many may not see it as their role to be suggesting new areas for business development, or they may see this as incidental. This may be partly related to the role expectations set by their discipline, and partly to the organization. Yet a finance director may be particularly well placed to identify possible profit-making opportunities.

In addition, they may not see the position as a consultancy role. More typically, the finance director's function may be seen as a controlling role, hardly conducive to a consultancy style. Further, the burden of regulatory requirements may drive out other value-adding activities. (Of course, this in itself may be said to add value purely by keeping the organization in business.)

A typical pattern is thus one where the individual (like many a business) lacks a clear focus on "what business they are in" and "where they can add most value." This lack of focus means that, while they are able to satisfy more routine demands, they suffer from an acute lack of time and energy with which to deviate to activities of a more strategic nature, which may add more value. As a result, they may begin to lack personal competitive advantage and thus become a "me-too" player in the organization.

The following exercise gives you a chance to reflect on added-value issues in relation to your own organizational role.

EXERCISE – UNDERSTANDING HOW YOU CAN ADD (MORE) VALUE (10 MINS)

1 What value do you generate in your own organizational role and in what key processes?
2 How can you reshape your role to add more (possibly *distinctive*) value?
3 What does this suggest about how you can develop your personal competitive advantage?

Following the above exercise you may have identified some key shifts that you can make, as well as some key priorities. In order to achieve these shifts in "how you do things around here," you may need to program how you can *stop doing* things that do not add value and *start doing* things that add very high value.

One of the most difficult parts of all, however, is to stop doing things that actually *destroy value*. If we return to our notional case of the finance director, we can think of a number of ways in which they may destroy value, for example by:

» adopting an excessively tight approach to financial controls, which results in gross inflexibility;
» imposing over-complex financial controls (e.g. in authorizing investment or costs);
» slowing down the decision-making process to a snail's pace;

» intimidating champions of new and valuable ideas; and
» adopting a policing, rather than a consulting, role.

The next exercise gives you the opportunity to reflect on those areas in which you may be destroying value.

EXERCISE – UNDERSTANDING HOW YOU CAN DESTROY VALUE (5 MINS)

1 How are you inadvertently destroying value in your organization?
2 What causes you to do this?
3 Is it your personal or professional style, or is this the way people customarily behave in the organization?
4 Is this because your role overlaps with that of other managers, or because tensions and conflicts are allowed to get out of hand?

An honest response to the above exercise should highlight at least one, and possibly several, areas where you are destroying value. The incidence of value destruction may be rife in the organization. This helps to explain why, when a well-focused 10–20% reduction in managers within an organization is combined with a shift in style and a refocusing of activities, little seems to suffer.

The analysis of how you create and destroy value in your organization leads us on to the next topic – identifying your personal competitive advantage.

WHAT IS YOUR PERSONAL COMPETITIVE ADVANTAGE?

Although the idea of competitive advantage is now widespread in management thinking, it has yet to crystallize in how individual managers think about their personal capability. Over the past few years, much energy has been expended on identifying and seeking to develop management competencies. But many of these initiatives have absorbed a great deal of analysis while the outputs have been slow to arrive, and are often cumbersome and usually cluttered to boot.

Effective management behavior is complex, but there may be a relatively small number of key ingredients that offer personal competitive advantage. These key ingredients may account for 80% of what may be a distinctive (as opposed to a mediocre) performance, yet account for only 20% of possible competencies (another example of the Pareto principle, previously mentioned in Chapter 2).

For instance, many managers contemplate, at some stage in their careers, "going independent as a management consultant." They may (erroneously) believe that the most critical competencies will be found in the area of functional skills and excellence. However, from a customer's point of view, these competencies are often regarded as merely getting the player into the game, as purely *enabling*. More *distinctive* skills of an independent consultant include:

» holistic vision – being able to see problems holistically, across functions and in their historical and political context;
» implementation focus – understanding the issues associated with implementing change in order to resolve problems, and displaying the skills of a *facilitator* as well as an *expert* in managing change;
» distinctive, interrelated skills – having a core of well-honed skills that form a *distinctive cluster* (i.e. they form part of a distinctive set);
» presentation of self – as an independent consultant you need to have, or develop, some sense of personal distinctiveness that fits your personal style and target clients (this might embrace becoming an acknowledged expert in a field in the public domain and finely honing your interpersonal skills so as to adapt "how you come over" according to individual client styles);
» networking – the ability to gather information and build relationships is crucial in order to help encourage people to come to you with their problems, as opposed to you having to chase around to find them with their problems; and
» flexibility – in order to provide a preferred alternative to the larger consulting firms, you need to develop flexibility that can allow you to respond in a more relevant and rapid mode.

You may wish to reflect now on how your own *enabling* competencies differ from your (possibly) *distinctive* competencies. Try the next exercise.

EXERCISE – UNDERSTANDING YOUR PERSONAL COMPETITIVE ADVANTAGE (20 MINS)

1 What are the sources of personal competitive advantage that *enable* you to execute your role competently using:
    i)   your functional skills?
    ii) your knowledge of how the business works?
    iii) your interpersonal skills?
    iv) your project/management skills?
    v)   your skills in planning and controlling resources?
    vi) your communication skills?

2 What are your sources of personal competitive advantage that give you a *distinctive* capability in:
    i)   your ability to look at problems cross-functionally and to analyze them strategically?
    ii) your leading-edge knowledge base (relevant to resolving key business problems)?
    iii) your leadership ability and strategic vision?
    iv) your competence in facilitating change?
    v)   your knowledge of the industry, your customers, competitors, suppliers, etc.?
    vi) your international experience and fluency in particular languages and culture?
    vii) your network of relationships such that you are influential at senior management level?

3 What are your key sources of personal *competitive disadvantage*? For instance, do you have:
    i)   specific skills where you are weak in areas that are regarded as fundamental by the customers who in effect buy your services?
    ii) a mainly single-functional vision?
    iii) major knowledge gaps (e.g. in marketing, IT, or finance?)
    iv) lack of exposure to how things are done elsewhere in the organization?
    v)   low awareness of how other companies work, especially in your field of expertise?

vi) lack of experience of front-line management (relevant to advisory staff who may not appreciate the pressures that line managers often face)?

vii) acute aversion to risk and to making errors?

viii) a tendency to deny or oversimplify problems?

ix) an apparent inability to plan more than a few months ahead?

Having worked through these questions using the various points as a checklist, you may now be in a better position to get some fix on "where you are now." Besides areas of distinctive advantage, you may also have pinpointed areas of personal competitive disadvantage. Just one of these areas of disadvantage may in effect eliminate you from significant upward or horizontal career progression.

For instance, your experience base may be too narrow if you have spent a long time in a single function or area of the business. Or you may have had a succession of roles that were not very demanding and so have not prepared you for the quantum leap to a general management role, or to head up a significant functional area. For organizations that are more process- or project-based, personal competitive disadvantage can be equally debilitating.

Outputs from these exercises should now help you to build or adapt your strategy for career development.

STRATEGIES FOR CAREER AND INDIVIDUAL DEVELOPMENT

Based on our contact with a large number of managers at both senior and middle levels, it would appear that relatively few individuals have formulated a clearly considered career strategy. This situation is beginning to change, partly due to the major restructurings of the 1990s and the early 2000s. These have made many managers reflect at greater length, although often in an all-structured way, on where their career paths are heading.

For many, this chapter may provide the first formal opportunity to explore your career options in a structured way. This involves looking at how these options fit with your personal competitive advantages, your development opportunities, and your personal values. This process will also help those (probably few) managers who have given this topic considerable thought, giving them the chance to refine and possibly refocus their strategy.

As we have hinted, development opportunities may occur which lead roughly (although rarely explicitly) in the direction of the career objective. However, where a manager decides on an opportunistic route, it can end up being a cul-de-sac. The "once-in-a-lifetime" experience may rapidly turn into a nightmare. This invites a personal illustration with which many managers may empathize.

CAREER STRATEGY – A CAUTIONARY TALE

During the middle of my own career, I confess to making one such mistake. I joined an organization to perform a role that, on the surface, fitted exactly with my strategic career objective in terms of the type of work; the type of company; the geographical location; the seniority and attendant package; my immediate boss; and so on. At the time, I felt some concerns about the move.

For instance, during the interview my future employers seemed very keen on my joining the company, but subsequently they seemed to take an unreasonably long time to offer me the position. I began to wonder what was happening behind the scenes. Did this role really exist? And if it did, what politics were going on to make the role such an evident football? Was I suffering from corporate paranoia, or were my natural instincts telling me something I would be unwise to ignore?

There also seemed to be a degree of confusion during my interview – could I please wait while they dragged a senior consultant away from finalizing a report (which looked like a last-minute panic) to talk to me? Was this a sign that this consulting firm had a very much less-organized style than the one I was accustomed to? You may recognize these symptoms from some of your own career move experiences.

Like many other managers, I had these concerns but I allowed them to be dampened by what seemed to be the obvious strategic fit of the move, not to mention dissatisfaction with where I was then. (Sometimes, however, it pays to listen to the stomach rather than the heart – or even the head – in assessing a new role.)

In my case it was not long (two to three months) before the gap between my job aspirations and the organizational reality that I faced in the new role was fully evident. Not only was the nature of the role different to what I had been led to believe, but the consulting work actually being done was a very different mix and the business unit lacked the critical skills to compete in the market. Yet, outwardly, all of these things seemed to have been in place.

After nine months, when I had received no response to my protestations about false expectations being raised, I resigned. The comment from a senior manager in the organization was interesting: "But you didn't come to tell us that you were so discontented; we had no inkling that you were about to resign. And we just put you as project leader of a major client review. . . ."

You may be interested to hear what happened subsequently. Two years after I left, the business unit was effectively dissolved following the early onset of recession. The heroic strategy of the business unit to grow into an "attractive" consulting niche (where it had little real competitive advantage) was a total failure. Wave after wave of reorganizations, redundancies, and redeployments were not enough to save the doomed unit.

The lessons of this experience are several.

1 Never let yourself be talked into a career move of dubious benefit while under the influence of profound, but possibly temporary, dissatisfaction with "where you are now."

2 If you do make a career mistake, you may find that it is better to pull the rug quickly rather than let the situation drag on. (Within no time, your new organization will bleat loudly that you haven't really tried hard and for long enough. You may also feel increasingly committed, even though your commitment is to the wrong thing.)

3 When moving organizations in the same industry, never assume that the culture and style of working will be more or less the same. (These could be radically different in subtle ways that seem arbitrary and often counter-productive.)

4 Sometimes it is better to defer a career move, so that you can take a bigger step later rather than accept something that may seem to be a fairly good fit but may well be a compromise.

5 Regardless of any misfit, always see what you can salvage out of a move of this kind, in terms of experience, skills, development, and personal contacts. (In this particular case, the year that the author spent was used to great value in developing the skills to become an independent strategy consultant.)

In order to cope with problems of career path uncertainty, one useful approach is to tell some scenario stories about a future career role or about the wider target organization. Another approach is to reflect on a past career move.

EXERCISE – REFLECTING ON A PAST CAREER MOVE (10 MINS)

For one career move made either within your existing organization or between organizations, reflect on the following.

1 To what extent was this part of a longer-term career strategy, or was it essentially opportunistic?

2 Did this matter either way? What were the benefits, costs, and risks?

3 What options did this particular career move open up (e.g. in terms of future career moves)?

4 How did it help you develop compared to what you expected?

5 If you were to go back in time and repeat the experience, what things (if any) would you have done differently?

Obviously, your own organization may have played a role in shaping this move, if it was an internal role. This raises the whole issue of what to do when a senior manager approaches you with "the offer you can't refuse." In many organizations it is still expected by managers, especially at middle level, that "if they ask you to do something, you do it." Yet you may even not be competent to do the thing that they ask. A not-uncommon scenario is for subtle (or less subtle) psychological pressure to be brought to bear.

For instance, at the age of 25, one of the authors was asked to apply for a senior finance job in the Far East, when he wanted a corporate planning job at group center of a major company. The response was, "But it really is a very nice place, you can take your family – it is hot and the pay is good. And remember, we won't forget you, as you will still be on London's books." This author's boss had evidently forgotten, in extolling the virtues of this particular country, that he had been there on business two months earlier. The boss had also forgotten that the author's wife was at university in the UK and that the author himself had wanted a job at the center precisely so that he wouldn't be forgotten at such an early juncture by London!

This may seem an extreme example, but it does highlight how critical it is for the individual to own their career.

This leads on to thinking strategically about various future career options. Figure 6.2 looks at two key variables – the degree of shift in style versus role. (Incidentally, the idea for this graph came

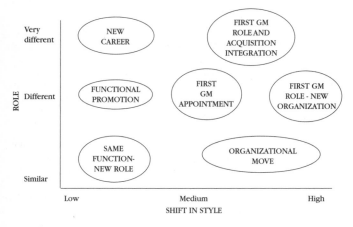

Fig. 6.2   Managing career transitions.

from other strategic tools, especially the analysis of existing versus new products and markets when comparing new business development opportunities.)

Figure 6.2 shows some examples of role moves to give an idea of how radical the shifts can be. For instance, a move within a similar functional role in the same organizational unit will be at the bottom left-hand corner of the matrix. A promotion in the same organization within function may be midway, but to the left. However, a promotion into general management (GM) will be to the very center. This may involve a significantly different *style* of managing.

Continuing this analysis, a move to another organization could involve a different or possibly very different style from what you have been accustomed to. A move from a specific function to a GM role across organizations could be midway up and to the right. Stretching these options even further, a first experience in GM involving at the same time the integration of an acquisition or, say, a turnaround job, would be to the far top-right corner. Many companies in the past saw their "bright young things" (possibly with an MBA or accounting qualification) going in at the deep end to integrate a new business. Sometimes this works and sometimes it doesn't; at any rate it is high risk.

Finally, a new career altogether might involve a very different role, and a similar or different style. For instance, someone moving from line management into consulting, or from consulting into a more academic role, may find this a very different career. Yet each crossing of a boundary may seem to be quite a small step, until afterwards. These positionings are illustrative, rather than definitive, and they need to be interpreted on a case-by-case basis.

It is now appropriate to look at your own longer-term career strategy, and consider how you will manage your career transitions, via the next exercise. We have already covered some of the key ingredients for this exercise, such as understanding how you add or destroy value in your current role, as well as understanding your personal competitive advantage. This defines your *current* position.

In the exercise, you should try to picture yourself at some *future* point in your career. This might be three, five, or possibly eight years into the future, depending on how far you have progressed into your career, and what options are suggested by your personal and organizational context. For instance, if you are a "fast mover" and are at an early stage in your career, you may wish to look at a three-year horizon within your current organization, possibly alongside some five-year options outside it. If you are somewhere on a career plateau, then you may need to start thinking about the possibility of a new career in, say, five or eight years' time. (This assumes a relatively stable environment.) Or, if the organization faces rapid change, it may be sensible to collapse these timescales and think about embarking on a new career strategy within one to two years, or less.

Now, try to answer the questions in the following exercise, as they are important. Don't just skim on to the next section, but do spend 20–30 minutes pondering your options. Return to these questions when you are next in a traffic jam or otherwise immobilized. Use your "dead time" to advantage by reflecting strategically on your career.

EXERCISE – SETTING A PERSONAL CAREER STRATEGY (20–30 MINS)

1 How is your own organization changing and developing over the timescale of your career strategy?
2 How do these changes and developments fit your current capabilities and those that you want to develop?
3 What specific opportunities and threats may be posed to your career within the organization? (Try to think both long-term and short-term.)
4 What does an analysis of your personal competitive advantage suggest in the way of opportunities elsewhere that may fit your capabilities?
5 How do these relate to your style of working, personal values, and personal life generally (including long-buried aspirations that you might (still) like to fulfill)?
6 What competencies would you need to develop in order to enhance your career through options within the organization or elsewhere?
7 How difficult would it be to develop these competencies (and within sufficient time to be able to exploit the opportunity in question)?

8 What could go wrong with a particular career option? How could you find out more in order to assess the risks, and gain more flexibility should these risks crystallize?

9 How do these options compare with that of following your existing (or a similar) career path, while making the very best of what you already have?

10 If you consider that you have already fulfilled your career strategy, what new challenge do you feel you might now fruitfully seek?

This exercise involves generating and assessing strategic options. It involves looking at your objectives and values, doing internal and external analysis, and analyzing your personal competitive position. It entails evaluating the key opportunities and threats, and also indicates how easy or difficult it will be to implement a number of strategic options, and with what results. In fact, it is one of the crimes of modern business thinking that "strategy" has become associated primarily (if not exclusively) with strategy at the corporate or business levels rather than at the personal level. For the individual manager, it can yield some quite powerful and immediate insights.

As a result of the above exercise, you may now have gained insights similar to those listed below.

1 While you have enjoyed working in your current organization, you are offered a quiet cul-de-sac at best as far as your career development is concerned. At worst, your comfortable position may evaporate owing to pending organizational change.

2 A new opportunity may have suggested itself through a move within the organization or elsewhere, but when subjected to closer scrutiny it does not really fit with your underlying aims, abilities, or values.

3 For some time you have considered the idea of a different career, but now you realize that you must make the jump soon or you may begin to appreciate how difficult such a move might be and decide to freeze the idea.

4 You may have come to the conclusion that, inadvertently, you are in danger of becoming stuck in a particular career rut, perhaps within a

particular function. It may now be time to make active steps towards, say, securing a GM position.

Following this exploration of your career options, let us now turn to the issue of managing career transitions.

HOW WILL YOU IMPLEMENT A CAREER TRANSITION?

Implementing a career strategy or a more tactical career move may give rise to the problem of managing a career transition. A career transition involves a major personal change. This change may go through a cycle of:

1 expectation-building – often of the exciting opportunities offered by the change;
2 disappointment – when these expectations are partially met, or are dashed;
3 adaptation – to the new environment, through modifying your style; and
4 consolidation – of your new role, by routinizing the things that are working.

This cycle can be protracted in duration, especially if you have not explicitly identified the transition as a learning process.

So how is it possible to manage career transition as a learning process? Let us begin by re-examining a past experience of a significant career transition.

EXERCISE – REFLECTING ON A MAJOR CAREER TRANSITION IN THE PAST (10 MINS)

Think back to a major career transition that you went through in the past.

1 Was this a success or a failure, or very much a mixed picture?
2 To what extent was this outcome affected by whether you *explicitly* saw this transition as a learning process?

3 With hindsight, what would you have done differently in managing this career transition?

4 What lessons can you draw for future or current career transitions?

In answering these questions, there may be issues such as the following that you wish to consider.

» Did you understand the degree to which you saw the transition as a major discontinuity, requiring different skills and recipes from those that had worked well in past roles?

» Did you avoid premature action to deliver quick results in the interest of performing a fuller diagnosis of the issues surrounding your new role?

» Did you get a clear picture of any stakeholders who might impact on these issues, and how you might influence them?

» Did you then manage the stakeholders' expectations of what, when, and how you would deliver?

Let us continue by looking at the key factors that *enable* and *constrain* a career transition.

EXERCISE – EXPLORING THE ENABLING AND CONSTRAINING FACTORS IN A CAREER TRANSITION (10 MINS)

For either a current/potential career transition or a past career transition, ask yourself the following.

1 Can you identify the key factors that would *enable* the career transition?

2 Can you identify the key factors that would *constrain* the career transition?

3 Are any of these factors likely to have a high, medium, or low impact on achieving an effective transition?

4 If the transition is a current/potential one, how might you now reconfigure these factors to make the process of transition more effective? (Note: Give considerable thought to new factors or influences that you might bring into play.)

DETAILED EVALUATION OF CAREER STRATEGIES

The strategic options grid (Table 6.1) is a useful way of evaluating both new job opportunities and career changes. This can be achieved by examining a number of possible future career routes against the criteria of:

» strategic attractiveness;
» financial attractiveness;
» implementation difficulty;
» uncertainty and risk; and
» acceptability to stakeholders.

Each of these criteria can be scored as high (3 ticks), medium (2 ticks), and low (1 tick) in terms of appeal. (Note: high implementation difficulty should be given 1 tick, and likewise high uncertainty and risk.)

For example, if we take the case of a young chartered accountant (aged 28) contemplating different career options, these might include:

» financial control/directorship of a strategic business unit;
» corporate treasury;

Table 6.1 Strategic options grid.

Criteria	Option 1	Option 2	Option 3	Option4
Strategic attractiveness				
Financial attractiveness*				
Implementation difficulty				
Uncertainty and risk				
Acceptability to stakeholders				

*Benefits less costs, relative to investment.

» acquisitions and mergers (merchant banking); or
» management consultancy.

These options can now be appraised using Table 6.1. Whilst financial control/directorship scores high on financial attractiveness, medium on strategic (or longer-term) attractiveness and on implementation difficulty, and low on uncertainty and risk, for this particular person the career is also low on acceptability. This is because the thought of a more traditional, mainly reporting role is less of a turn-on. (A score of 11 overall.)

On the other hand, a career in corporate treasury is strategically unattractive and very difficult, counterbalanced by being very attractive financially, low in uncertainty, and highly acceptable. (A score of 11 overall.)

A career in acquisitions and mergers scores very high on strategic and financial attractiveness, and on acceptability to this stakeholder, but is highly uncertain and of medium difficulty. (A score of 12 overall.)

Finally, a management consultancy career is highly attractive strategically and highly acceptable, but of medium financial attractiveness, medium difficulty, and high risk. (A score of 11 overall.)

So, by a narrow margin, a career in acquisitions and mergers comes out as the best option. But hold on a minute – if this person was relatively risk-averse, a high-risk career in acquisitions and mergers might be less appealing than a low-risk career in either corporate treasury or financial control/directorship.

Because of the emotional sensitivity of difficult career choices, it is imperative to use some form of quasi-objective technique like the strategic options grid to discriminate between options. The technique allows some of the trade-offs to be examined, and will help to test out underlying assumptions and values.

EXERCISE – WORKING ON YOUR OWN CAREER STRATEGY (ONCE AGAIN!)

For a number of career options or, more specifically, job roles that you have in mind, try and answer the following questions.

1 How do these rate on the strategic options grid?
2 Given the relative weight that you place on these different options, how does this affect your overall view of the relative attractiveness of these options?

SUMMARY

In this chapter, we have explored how all managers need to reflect at length on their personal strategic capability and career strategy. This can be achieved by:

» thinking hard about career moves, not merely in terms of the value of the immediate move, but also the value of things it might lead to and things it might preclude;
» being continuously aware of how and whether you are adding concrete value to the organization;
» avoiding the destruction of value in your role (at all costs) even if this means fighting against organizational style;
» understanding what your key sources of personal competitive advantage are and continually building on them (particularly the distinctive ones);
» thinking about the fit of your bundle of personal competitive advantages and disadvantages with your current and potential roles; and
» having a deliberate, rather than just an emergent, strategy for developing your own career.

Success Stories

INTRODUCTION

In this chapter, we focus on three companies who have fostered individual development with outstanding success. The companies are:

1 Dowty Communications, who have used strategic learning to develop the organization;
2 Mercury Communications, who have used learning and development to improve operational and individual performance; and
3 Hewlett-Packard, who have used one-to-one strategy coaching to enhance general management skills in senior managers.

CASE STUDY 1 – DOWTY COMMUNICATIONS

This case study of Dowty Communications shows how strategic learning can simultaneously develop the business, the organization, and the key individuals within it.

Background

Dowty Communications (formerly Case Communications) was a rapidly growing entrepreneurial company based at Watford, England. It had achieved major and early success with wide area networks (WAN), and built a solid market position in the UK.

The company grew by spreading its business activities geographically, with more products, and through new distribution channels – becoming more complex.

A number of issues and agendas then conspired to crystallize a major attempt at strategic learning by Dowty. These issues and agendas included the following.

» The (new) managing director (MD) and his team faced the daily problem of sorting out which new business ideas to back and which to exclude. As the MD is reported to have said at the time, "I get at least one new business idea every day across my desk. We obviously can't do everything. But how do we justify our decisions?"
» There was encouragement from group for the MD to complete one "breakthrough" project. Conducting a strategic review would

help not only the top team deal with its medium- and longer-term aspirations, but would also fulfill the need to complete a breakthrough project.

Dave King, the newly appointed director of business development, was given the task of coordinating the strategic learning to deliver a strategic plan. As one of his personal objectives, this was on his critical path in fulfilling his new job role (and indeed of getting his Christmas bonus, which had been earmarked for a new Suzuki Trooper for his wife). This put Dave under significant pressure to "deliver a strategic plan" by a date in the early autumn, giving him a very clear action agenda to drive his learning.

The strategic review as a strategic learning process

Issues, tasks, and levels of involvement

Figure 7.1 illustrates the strategic learning process. This highlights the extent of involvement at directorial level and within the small team

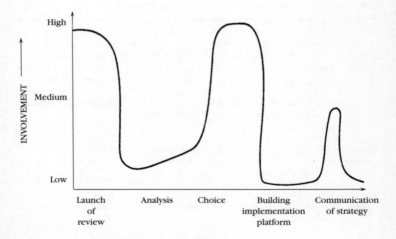

Fig. 7.1   Strategic learning – Directors' involvement.

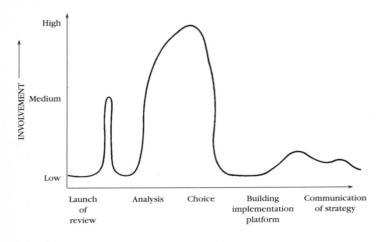

Fig. 7.2 Strategic learning – Senior managers' involvement.

Table 7.1 Involvement levels of key players in the strategic learning process.

	Directors	Facilitators	Senior managers
Analysis (June–August)	SWOT analysis	Tested SWOT analysis	Market potential
	Mission/goals	Distilled key strategic issues	Country analysis
	Individual to senior manager teams	Analyzed macro-options	Technology appraisal
			Business processes People capability
Choice (September)	Country decisions	Documenting rationale	No involvement (directly)
	Channel decisions Product decisions		
Implementation (December)	Individuals to lead projects	Project-management process	Workshops on managing change
			Possible involvement in projects

of core facilitators – Dave King (internally) and one of the authors (externally).

Figure 7.2 shows that although senior managers had a very substantial involvement in the strategic learning process, they did not have any real involvement directly in the choice phase. With hindsight, this phase might have been performed differently, to avoid the drop between thinking mode and implementation mode.

Table 7.1 gives a more detailed breakdown of the involvement levels of the key players.

KEY LESSONS

Much of the benefit of strategic learning came through managers changing their views of the organization and its environment. Learning often entails challenging assumptions.

Some of the key lessons of the strategic learning process are listed below. These initial lessons were learned both individually and as a team by the company's directors.

Analysis

» The company's markets were becoming less attractive owing to their greater maturity, competitive rivalry, and increased investment requirements.
» The company's competitive position was not as strong as had previously been believed. In a number of areas it had a competitive disadvantage.
» The range of business areas had become very complex, and in many areas the company lacked critical mass.
» A relatively small number of core activities accounted for almost all the business profit stream.
» There were symptoms of a backlog of undigested strategic change that had accumulated throughout the 1980s.

Choice

» The company needed to narrow its range of activities.

» Any new activities would need to be carefully screened against the existing strategies and against new business criteria.
» Some significant operational changes needed to be made in the UK.

Implementation
» The backlog of change was considerable and presented an even greater challenge than the earlier analysis and choice phases.

So what was learned about the learning process?

The Dowty Communications case is rich in lessons about the strategic learning process. These lessons have been distilled into the following points, which are explored in turn:

» infuse learning within and across the organization;
» build learning into "how we do things around here;"
» avoid overdosing and manage the "come-down;"
» strategic learning may well shift the existing power base
» involve the leader at the center of the process and build their learning capability;
» use communication as a vehicle for learning; and
» the successful facilitator must be an excellent learner.

Infuse learning within and across the organization

Unless strategic learning is infused within and across the organization, through workshops and project work, its impact will be rapidly blunted. In the Dowty Communications case this blunting occurred for the following two reasons.

1 The directors were initially involved during the analysis phase but then to no particularly great extent until the choice phase. Equally, senior managers were heavily involved during the analysis phase but were substantially excluded from the choice phase, and then expected to remobilize in the implementation phase. This all encourages unlearning.

2 Group management were excluded from the learning, so that business-level learning did not interface with corporate learning.

The effect of the first point above is graphically illustrated in Figures 7.1 and 7.2, which show the roller coaster of involvement levels of directors and senior managers respectively. Notice both the blips of involvement, how they occur at different times for directors versus senior managers, and the loss of momentum and delay prior to communicating the strategy. These curves were drawn after the event. We would advise anyone planning a major strategic learning exercise to sketch these in advance during their planning process!

The end product in terms of organizational learning is described by Dave King:

> "Yes, I am sure that very many people learned an awful lot about the organization at senior level, especially through the workshops helping them manage change issues. In fact, the insights were real, positively dangerously real at times."

Build learning into "how we do things around here"

All too often learning is associated with cerebral reflection that only has an indirect impact on real management activity. But learning can be incorporated into the processes that individuals carry out. At Dowty Communications, learning subsequently needed to be incorporated into management routines, such as those involving:

» strategic workshops;
» customer views;
» business measures;
» cost reduction/simplification;
» competitor analysis; and
» market analysis.

Avoid overdosing and manage the "come-down"

Strategic learning can be an exciting and intoxicating experience. It can also be very tiring, as it is strenuous to keep in double-loop learning mode for a sustained period of time. This means that managers need to pace themselves; it also highlights the need to make the learning process design no more complex than necessary.

The danger is that, with the core of learning completed, managers can step back into single-loop learning. But continued reflection and iteration may be required well into the implementation process.

The problem is akin to that of mobilizing an army for battle. Once this is achieved and the battle fought, the troops may want to demobilize rather than stay on a war footing. Having demobilized, the troops can be difficult to remobilize, except for minor exercises.

Strategic learning may well shift the existing power base

During the review, the influence of key players in the management team shifted as a result of their involvement. This indicates that learning is not a power-neutral process. Dave King illustrates this in looking at how the review was used within the directorial team and at senior management level:

> "What you may have a problem with is when you set something up trying to involve people ... when in fact you or others really believe there is a need to drive some particular things through."

Involve the leader at the center of the process and build their learning capability

Although it is a truism that the leader must be involved in a symbolic way and as a key stakeholder in a strategic review, making this happen is not always easy. Not only are there likely to be many other distractions for the MD/CEO, but there are a number of factors that may actively discourage a sufficiently deep involvement.

» The leader may feel increasingly uncomfortable about the process. Rather than become more involved, they may actually become less so, which in turn may heighten their discomfort.

» There may be valid concerns about not wanting to foreclose options prior to the choice phase.

» The leader may feel reluctant to admit that they are learning as the process proceeds, especially if strategic analysis or other tools are being utilized in which they are not fluent.

These factors may compound with others (such as "I am simply too busy anyway") to result in effective decoupling of the leader from the learning process.

Use communication as a vehicle for learning

In the Dowty Communications case, a major opportunity was missed by not inviting managers' input on the implementation requirements of the strategy, prior to the strategy's communication.

Again, communication in organizations can be a two-way interchange, yet in this instance the process was seen as cascading down rather than being two-way and iterative. Besides getting a clearer view of implementation issues, managers can also gain much greater ownership of the strategy.

The successful facilitator must be an excellent learner

A facilitator needs to be an excellent learner in order to be effective. Here are some tips.

» A facilitator should have patience in debating the process to make sure it is not "just about right" but that it is "absolutely right."
» The internal facilitator should have the ability to remain unswayed by personal views or pet ideas. Only then can the facilitator challenge groupthink. They also need to be able to use strategic frameworks, but be mindful of the need to filter these so as to avoid indigestion.
» The external facilitator should have the ability to learn very rapidly about the organization. They need to have a broad knowledge of the management disciplines concerned with "soft" as well as "hard" issues. Finally, they must be sufficiently flexible to blend with the needs of the management team but challenge core assumptions when the time is right.

Reflections and conclusions

The Dowty Communications case shows how individual and group organizational learning processes can be integrated and used to drive the business forward. In the course of this process significant development in capability can occur, not just at the organizational level but also at the individual level.

Dave King went on to senior business development roles in a larger telecommunications company, as well as moving on to strategy consultancy work within the industry. The author gained the confidence to develop strategy in larger and more challenging environments such as the British oil company BP, the British bank HSBC, the Finnish mobile phone company Nokia, the British financial services organization Standard Life, and the British supermarket chain Tesco.

During the case, the issue of using strategic learning to drive implementation became a recurrent theme. This theme is now much amplified by a case from a non-competing company in another part of the same industry – Mercury Communications.

CASE STUDY 2 – MERCURY COMMUNICATIONS

Background

Mercury Communications was, at the time of this case study, the subsidiary of the British multinational company. Mercury's operations were principally in the UK and Mercury had made major inroads into the UK telecommunications market. Mercury Communications had expanded extremely rapidly, reaching a turnover of well over £1bn by the mid-1990s.

This success story takes us right into the heart of Mercury Communications and into a key business unit, Mercury Messaging.

Mercury Messaging's senior team was already well advanced in devising a strategy for the future development of the business. Here the need was one of helping improve the quality of operations, particularly by improving organizational capability. The case is described as follows:

» origins and scope of the learning and development initiative;
» the learning and development process;
» making it happen;
» extracting the benefits; and
» lessons on orchestrating the learning and development process.

Origins and scope of the learning and development initiative

The general manager of Mercury Messaging, John Mittens, was becoming concerned about his staff's ability to implement the strategy, which was likely to stretch their capabilities much more than in the past. Many staff in the organization appeared to be focused on striving to be more efficient rather than more effective.

Very few staff had much formal management development – their training had been primarily of a sales or technical nature. Most worked long hours, some of which were spent in resolving tactical problems rather than trying to understand and rectify the underlying causes of these problems.

All these symptoms seemed to point to a major management skills gap in the organization, and there was a danger that this gap might widen when the organization tried to implement its strategy for further development. John Mittens and Mercury Messaging's HR manager, Russell Connor, met to discuss how they might tackle this issue. Russell's views of the problem were as follows:

> "We have a number of staff, particularly those whose backgrounds are mainly sales/technical, who we try to coach and direct but due to their limited experience they are often unable to come to grips with the basics of good management. For instance, when we pursue market opportunity they hardly seem to pause for breath before they are in the middle of the project. The result is that we have too many projects, many of which don't really fit with what we are trying to achieve overall. And the good ones we do have become disrupted when someone gets pulled off to do something more urgent.
>
> "Many of our staff are still relatively young and are in danger of continuing like this unless they can somehow switch over to a different way of managing."

A learning and development program was then put together to work on some live business issues. The program was underpinned by four aims.

1 It would not just involve individual learning but also team and organizational learning.
2 It would involve action-working on live issues with a view, subsequently, to implementing appropriate changes.
3 It would be business-focused, so that it would not just constitute action learning for the individuals involved, but would also help John Mittens solve some of Mercury Messaging's most important business issues.
4 It would be a modular program – not simply a course but a series of workshops and projects.

The learning and development process

The overall learning and development process is shown in Figure 7.3. Prior to the core workshops, further work was done to refine the key issues into a series of four questions, one for each of four learning and development projects.

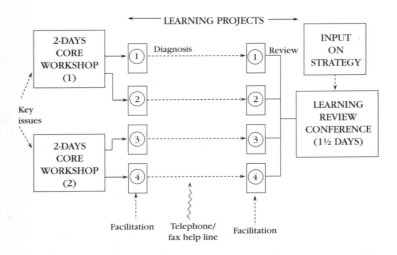

Fig. 7.3 The learning and development process.

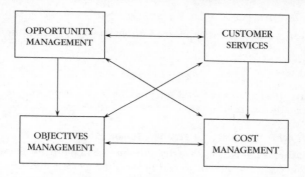

Fig. 7.4   Learning and development projects.

The four issues that were chosen (see Figure 7.4) were:

1 opportunity management;
2 objectives management;
3 cost management; and
4 customer services.

Figure 7.4 shows the four interdependent learning and development projects networked together. Each of the four projects was defined by a key question, as follows.

Learning project 1 – Opportunity management
How can we improve our process for identifying, screening, evaluating, deciding on, and finally programming:

» strategic opportunity?
» tactical opportunity?

What barriers to change would need to be surmounted to achieve this?

Learning project 2 – Objectives management
What should be the role of objectives (strategic, operational, and financial) in steering a path through future change, and how can these objectives be used to greater effect in the business?

Learning project 3 – Cost management

How can we reduce our expenses without damaging the business:

» short-term?
» long-term?

In what specific areas do you see possibilities for improving leverage between the use of resource and value added?

Learning project 4 – Customer services

In what areas can we improve the customer service process in order to generate further competitive and financial benefits at minimum cost, and what barriers to change might need to be overcome?

The core issue

Of these four learning and development projects, the core issue was that of opportunity management. This was an area with greatest potential impact on the business. It was also the area where *most change* was eventually accomplished.

The core workshops

About a dozen managers attended each of the two core workshops, which were run on alternate weeks and covered competitive change, financial awareness, and opportunity development.

Following the core workshops, each learning project team spent approximately half a week in group sessions working on the project issue. In addition, they also spent some individual time in further analysis. The workshops extended over a two and a half month period, and were facilitated by an independent consultant via a telephone/fax helpline, which was very actively used.

It was felt best to give the groups in each team between two and three months to work on their learning and development projects, as a shorter period would have not done justice to the issues and a longer period would probably have resulted in a loss of momentum.

Each project had a learning project plan and an appointed project coordinator. The managers were also given online access to John Mittens as key stakeholder and as mentor. In order to enhance learning on teamwork, all participants took the Belbin team role test (see Chapter 9 for more details). This proved very useful, not so much in stereotyping individuals as "only a plant," "only a shaper," or "only a chairman," but in encouraging individuals to develop those team roles that did not come quite as naturally to them.

The project activities culminated in a project review workshop. Here the outside facilitator provided input to test and reshape presentations, taking care not to over-facilitate and over-intrude on each team's ownership of outputs.

Finally, all four learning projects were presented at a review conference attended by all managers in a hotel at the top of Richmond Hill, London. This conference lasted an intensive one and a half days (beginning at five o'clock in the evening). The format for the presentations was:

1 the project outputs – "What we found out;"
2 the learning and development process – "What we learned about the process, tools, etc. and about wider organizational issues;"
3 debate and constructive critique; and
4 the facilitator's summary on the outputs *and* the process.

In addition, John Mittens was able to spend time formulating a strategic overview that put the projects into a wider context.

Mercury Messaging then decided to extend the learning and development process into a second phase. The four learning and development projects were relabeled as "change projects," signaling their transformation into high reality and into action.

Making it happen

John Mittens played a key role as sponsor in ensuring that the change projects did not terminate prematurely just after the Richmond Hill conference. It would have been very easy for him to have expected "things simply to happen," but he maintained an active involvement in the initial stages of implementation.

A number of *process* lessons emerged from the four projects.

» During the diagnosis stage, the definition of the problem changed quite considerably. In some cases, the scope of the problem (and thus the project) seemed to grow. Learning project teams need to understand that to a degree this is inevitable as they learn more about the issues and their underlying causes.

» Teams devoted at least half a day per week to the projects together (in addition to further investigations carried out individually). This put an additional burden on their workload. Again, it is essential to set their expectations realistically for the level of input required for the projects. It may be useful to couple this with a renewed effort in task effectiveness and time management in their day-to-day responsibilities. Also, at times it was difficult to get the teams together as a quorum because of other business pressures. This highlights the need to give (and sustain) a sufficiently high level of priority for the projects vis-à-vis other activities.

» Cynicism that management may not be serious about desiring change is highly likely to surface at some stage. Management need to be aware of these perceived discrepancies and be prepared to address them positively rather than compartmentalize them. Staff, in turn, need to manage any tendencies towards cynicism and put themselves in the position of more senior management who may seek to change behavior and management style, but quickly suffer relapse.

Extracting the benefits

The key benefits from the four change projects are detailed below.

Opportunity management

Mercury Messaging created a more formal and thorough process for screening and evaluating new product/market/technology opportunity. This involved not merely looking at the financial and sales projections but also the inherent strategic attractiveness of the opportunity externally, as well as taking into account Mercury Messaging's competitive position and the extent to which this could be sustained.

A series of bullet-point questions was drawn up and tested against past opportunities (good and not so good) in order to pilot the appraisal device. A common framework was adopted for both better screening and detailed evaluation, structured according to four key questions.

1 Is the market that the opportunity addresses inherently attractive, thereby offering above-average profitability?
2 Do we have competitive advantage and can we sustain this?
3 Will the financial returns be sufficient?
4 Given our resources and capability, can we implement it effectively?

This process was facilitated by the declaration of a "learning amnesty," in which Mercury Messaging managers could be totally open about lessons from past projects without fear of retribution.

Objectives management

Progress on this particular issue was slightly more difficult to achieve. The project team and senior management agreed that staff ought to have a clearer framework of individual and team objectives, linked to business objectives. They also agreed on the *content* of these objectives. What was more difficult, however, was resolving the issue of *flexibility*.

On the one hand, Mercury Messaging wanted to preserve as much flexibility of goals and objectives as possible but, on the other hand, everyone realized that taken to an extreme this fluidity made it more difficult to achieve goals owing to ever-changing priorities. This feature is by no means unique to Mercury Messaging; to a lesser or greater extent, all organizations face this dilemma. When a company is grappling with major external (and internal) change, this dilemma can become acute.

Cost management

Although the members of this team had a particularly difficult time at the early diagnosis stage, they went on to produce some very useful insights and identified a number of areas for more effective cost management. The following were some of the key outputs from the project.

» A number of areas were identified where *cost monitoring systems* could be significantly improved.
» A much more *cost-aware* culture was created where staff began to challenge, continuously, whether objectives could be achieved with less cost.

» In one specific area, the potential for some *very major cost savings* was highlighted.

Customer services

This project concerned a mixture of customer-focus, organizational, and cost issues. The project team had to ensure that they retained a clear focus throughout, as a result of this diversity of issues. Nevertheless, it proved possible to crystallize a number of options for refocusing and concentrating the resources of Mercury Messaging's customer services activities.

KEY LESSONS

The Mercury Communications case yields lessons on applying strategic learning in three key areas:

1 business outputs;
2 organizational outputs; and
3 the learning process.

Business outputs

» Learning can be a powerful way of refocusing how an organization facing complex choices (as was the case with Mercury Messaging) deals with new business opportunity and all of its key individual managers.
» It can also generate some major cost savings without damaging competitive advantage.

Organizational outputs

» Although at Mercury Messaging the attempt to develop a framework for objectives did not appear to deliver its intended outputs, the real benefits were obtained through management realizing that a formal framework would not be workable.

» One of the key benefits of a learning and development process spanning the organization like this can be that of team development. In the Mercury case the managers got to know each other much better through the cross-functional project teams, building a career culture, and this proved to be an important benefit.

The learning process

» Strategic learning programs need the active and symbolic involvement of the top managers (as was the case at Mercury Messaging).
» Sometimes the outputs from the learning process are unexpected. For instance, at Mercury Messaging a workable framework of objectives did not materialize, but managers learned to work more closely with one another. This resulting improvement in communication did a great deal to resolve the problem.
» The benefits of learning and development can often lag behind the initial intervention.
» An energy dip can occur when individuals get too engrossed in developmental activities. This stems from the "Can I now go back to my main job?" syndrome. Learning and development programs of this kind can make intensive demands on managers' energies. Energy levels should not become too depleted.
» The value of learning and development is sometimes hard to assess because much of the value is generated through intermingling with other initiatives but, as part of a wider set, the value is very real.

Lessons on orchestrating the learning and development process

The Mercury Communications case highlights the very tangible benefits of strategic learning and also reinforces previous lessons on orchestrating the learning and development process in a particularly testing environment, as follows.

» Learning and development initiatives should be very clearly targeted.
» These targets can embrace learning, specific change, and shifts in organizational style at an individual, team, and company level.
» The process needs to be well positioned and consistently supported by top management.
» The process requires skilful facilitation.

The case study also shows again that individual development cannot easily be divorced from the organizational processes, style, and culture within which the individual is working. If a sustained intervention is created to shift this context, individuals can develop much more positively and confidently than with narrow, individually focused development activities.

CASE STUDY 3 – HEWLETT-PACKARD

Background

A newly appointed senior manager at the American electronics and computing manufacturer Hewlett-Packard (HP) – whom we will call Lauren Blackwell – was looking at all of her issues one day and caught herself thinking:

> "There are just so many things to deal with. And the really big issues I never seem to have sufficient time for. I am being inundated by reports asking me to deal with issues that they should be able to deal with on their own. I feel the lack of any formal management to date is beginning to prevent me from getting on top of this. But I really don't have time to spend three weeks on a formal general management program. And I would also love to be able to deal with these issues more privately and with some independent and honest input."

In conversation with the head of management development, she was advised to spend some sessions with an independent strategy coach. Lauren had returned to HP after maternity leave in an unusual way. She was ironing at home and the telephone rang. It was her former boss. "Lauren," he said, "I am sorry to disturb you at home but I have some news. I have just been appointed head of Europe. You wouldn't happen to want to think about coming back sooner and taking on my job, would you?''

It was an opportunity too great for Lauren to let slip by, and so she resumed work but in a job she might not have anticipated.

The main issues that Lauren faced were:

» putting out day-to-day operational fires;
» managing and meeting sales targets;
» developing a more effective business strategy;
» establishing her own role and setting her expectations of her staff;
» dealing with certain areas of organizational rivalry; and
» personal time management.

Initial strategy coaching

Lauren then met with a strategy coach for three one-day sessions, each spaced about four weeks apart. These sessions were structured as follows.

Session 1
» Familiarization with Lauren's career, skills, and style.
» Problem-solving techniques – and their application.
» Prioritization of problems/issues.
» Work on Lauren's time management.

Session 2
» Sales targets and gap analysis.
» Dealing with organizational rivalry.
» Managing subordinates – and communication with them.
» Further improvements to time management.

Session 3
» Strategic thinking and options.
» Implementing strategy.
» Working on Lauren's strategy.
» Next development steps.

Results

The results of this strategy coaching were substantial. Lauren had a number of really big wins.

» Her ability to diagnose and evaluate problems, and suggest appropriate solutions, improved quickly and considerably.
» She was able to resolve certain difficulties of internal rivalry, which could have dragged on and been highly distracting.
» Lauren cleared about 20% of her diary for strategic thinking space, and was more able to spend sufficient time with her family.
» Lauren's confidence grew tangibly.

Further strategy coaching

From time to time, Lauren involved her strategy coach at a number of key junctures. For instance, she sought his input when developing two account strategies for major companies so as to help meet long-term sales targets. Also, some time after, she sought out his help in dealing with one very major dilemma that had been bothering her. By that stage Lauren had been promoted *twice*, and now had approximately 20,000 people reporting to her globally.

In 2001, Lauren reflected on that issue, which had proven to be intractable:

"It just completely wipes you out, in terms of your ability to concentrate on the day job. And in my job a lot of it is about motivating people. People read every little sign, and if your mind is somewhere else, they know straight away. They interpret the signals as all sorts of things. So, that was worrying, and most of my team had spotted it. They were engaged in it, and the whole organization became paralyzed. This had been going on for several weeks.

"That issue was a festering, gaping sore. Just sitting down and going through that with a coach, just taking me through that strategic options grid [see Table 6.1] and taking me out of my day job, it put the whole thing in context."

Dealing with this issue as a learning process, supported by coaching, enabled Lauren to be reflective, dispassionate, and ultimately confident in pursuing the way ahead. One of the key benefits that Lauren singled out as being of tangible value in the strategy coaching was her greater confidence in the area of strategic thinking:

> "Just taking a day out to do strategic thinking does make a difference, out of the day-to-day environment. Often, and this is what it is like for most people in a sales organization, you end up with weekly, quarterly, annual pressure and targets. And you get really stuck into those – the grunt and grind, and the minutiae. And you don't get a chance to step back.
>
> "It's that helicopter thing. Getting up in the helicopter and looking down. The thought that you are someone from Mars and have landed on Earth and don't have a clue – it gives you a completely fresh view. Looking from above – sometimes you catch yourself doing it. Sometimes I catch myself doing it in a meeting. I let them get on with it, and I go up, up. I have a look and listen. It is really good practice; you look at things from a completely different angle.
>
> "So, being able to go up in the helicopter often, and then to come back and land on the ground, it seems to be pretty unusual to have that ability. People cannot seem to jump the divide."

Lauren's view of strategic thinking was very pragmatic (which might have been difficult to obtain from a more formal course):

> "In today's world, you know, we don't get a minute! But we can get a minute. With the e-mails and the Internet, and communication at every time of the day and night, the pace is getting faster and faster and faster – you don't get time to implement far-fetched or too academic or too theoretical ideas. You have got to be quick."

Lauren felt strongly that strategic thinking (and, by implication, her strategy coaching) had been uniquely beneficial:

> "Well, helicopter thinking has done me good, because it has helped make lots of career moves for me [laughs]. So, somewhere

along the line one must see some correlation. I think helicopter thinking must have been one of the contributory factors. There are not a lot of people around who can balance the strategic and the tactical. There are a lot of people who can be very tactical, and there is another group of people who can be quite strategic. But getting the two things to come together is quite difficult.''

One major advantage of the strategy coaching process was that it didn't just focus on one key dimension of development, such as strategic thinking. It was sufficiently flexible to cover implementation and change management skills, and the handling of resistances, as well.

Lauren summed up her views on the value of the overall process and, in particular, on the benefits of using an external strategy coach rather than an internal mentor:

''You need someone to bounce your ideas off, because you need some help to get out of the context into a more objective way of thinking. Or, just to get somebody to give you a different view.

''You could use somebody from inside the company I guess, a mentor or a coach. A relationship and trust would be needed. But I probably couldn't have dealt with that issue without getting some partiality, and avoid potential leakage as well. With most things which are really important, news travels really fast in our organization. You don't want to be sharing your thought process with someone who can pass on what your thinking is. You could find that the ideas turn into something which you hadn't intended, or might get misinterpreted, or have implications in the business – you need to get outside.''

KEY LESSONS

The key lessons from this short case on Lauren Blackwell's success at HP are as follows.

» Formal management development might be too generic and inflexible to help upgrade general management skills.

» One-to-one support can accelerate development, and help to integrate learning and action directly and quickly.
» The payback period for learning and development can be very short indeed, in both personal and financial terms. (Just think what could have gone wrong organizationally if Lauren had never acquired the "helicopter" view of things.)
» Strategy coaching is best approached by having an initially structured and programmed series of sessions – which provide a focus, a discipline, and a critical learning mass – followed by more occasional, just-in-time, and generally shorter inputs.
» Where the individual is already in a very senior position, it is often better and more appropriate to use an external strategy coach rather than an internal mentor.

SUMMARY

» At Dowty Communications, strategic learning helped the organization, its top team, and its key individuals to develop their vision and capability considerably, and delivered a strategic plan.
» At Mercury Communications, learning and development were used to transform operational management, performance, and capability, enabling individuals to be genuinely more empowered and successful.
» At HP, strategy coaching enabled Lauren Blackwell to develop her capability and career not only within HP but also subsequently as managing director of a technology company.

Key Concepts and Thinkers

INTRODUCTION

There are a variety of perspectives on how the individual uses learning as a period for development. These begin with David Kolb, who argued that learning goes through a series of cycles, from having concrete experiences, through reflecting on the experiences and building concepts, to testing out the learning in practice.[1] Kolb's model is relatively simple, and we expand this model into the more complex and stretching forms of learning known as *strategic learning*.

We then look at Peter Honey and Alan Mumford's notion that different individuals have different learning styles,[2] and the implications for how individuals manage and plan their development. The *action learning* approaches of Reg Revans[3] and Malcolm Knowles[4] are examined next.

Chris Argyris then helps us to look at how learning on the job tends to short-circuit when managers are faced with uniquely challenging situations, getting stuck in *single-loop* versus *double-loop learning*.[5] This is captured in the polar-opposite metaphors of "rabbit-hole" and "helicopter" thinking.

We then analyze the contribution to *systems thinking* made by Peter Senge,[6] and consider how relevant this is for the individual. Senge's concepts are made concrete in our section on *scenarios* as a vehicle for learning.

Finally, the role of *neurolinguistic programming* in developing the individual is explored, with reference to the work of John Grinder and Richard Bandler.[7]

LEARNING AS FEEDBACK – DAVID KOLB

Kolb is a major thinker in learning and development. Kolb differentiated between four phases of learning for the individual, namely:

1 *concrete experience* – interaction with the world, often of a social or symbolic nature (e.g. a failed acquisition);
2 *reflective observation* – absorbing the results of this interaction, and interpreting its meaning and causality (e.g. "the biggest difficulties were in acquisition integration 12 months in");
3 *abstract conceptualization* – fitting the experience into a wider conceptual framework, and making inductive generalizations

(e.g. "these difficulties were caused by not having a sufficiently thought-through integration plan, inappropriate interventions in operations, and senior staff leaving"); and

4 *active experimentation* – testing the conceptual framework and generalizations in new situations (e.g. building into future acquisition plans contingency for integration difficulties; more advanced integration planning; project management; deployment of experienced integrators; and use of an integration task force drawn from the acquired company's management).

These four stages are shown in the learning cycle in Fig. 8.1.

Kolb's framework is thus a dynamic model of learning in which the learning cycle is continuously recurring. Kolb therefore suggests that learning is not rigid (i.e. having an input process followed by an output process), but is fluid and iterative. At any stage in time the product of learning is likely to be incomplete, and learning gaps will still be discovered in new experiences and situations.

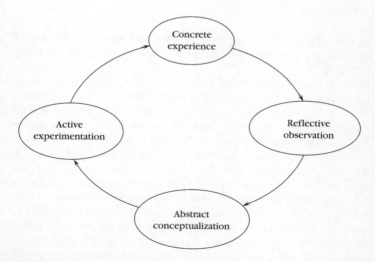

Fig. 8.1   Kolb's learning cycle.

Kolb suggests that whilst an individual normally moves through their learning processes sequentially and in a clockwise direction, they will sometimes need to go back to the earlier stages. For example, in concrete experience or active experimentation, the individual might also be engaged in abstract conceptualization (checking out their models of the world).

It is also possible for the learning cycle to become blocked. This can occur as follows.

» Whilst an individual is in concrete experience, they may not observe things that are going on. Also, they may fail to reflect on these things (either enough or at all).
» Some reflective observation may be done, but abstract conceptualization may only be done in so far as observations are fitted into pre-existing mental maps. New abstract conceptualization, and thus real learning, may fail to occur.
» Abstract conceptualization may occur, but there may be a failure to translate this into active experimentation (with the new concepts or generalizations).

In particular, where a problem is identified, this may be denied, or considered insoluble at present and laid on the shelf for future reflection.

The ability of an individual to move through the four stages effortlessly, quickly, and effectively has been described as "learning to learn" by Honey and Mumford.[8] *Learning to learn* can be defined as "the consciousness that learning is going on, and the process of discovering which learning strategies may enhance that learning."

Interestingly many, if not most, individuals are much worse at learning to learn than they are at simpler forms of learning. For example, at management courses on strategic thinking most managers can only come up with 10–15% of the potential learning lessons from a case study, *even when these lessons have been brought out explicitly during group feedback and debate on the case study.* Learning to learn is not merely a theoretical concept, but is also a very important management competency. It is associated particularly with top management and with the identification of high-flyers.

Learning to learn helps to accelerate individual development by building competence in a more efficient way. For instance, one of the benefits of doing an MBA is that an individual's ability to absorb and reflect upon data is much improved. A good MBA student will learn quickly which frameworks to apply to what, how to get more out of them, and how best to deploy such tools when up against quite new sets of data. An excellent MBA student will be able to evolve new concepts by combining existing frameworks in new ways, thus generating insights and options that even their tutor might not have anticipated. Active experimentation can thus be linked to abstract conceptualization through conceptual experimentation. This is often the source of new and innovative thinking.

Kolb's model focuses primarily on the individual interacting with an environment, learning how to get things done better or to get new things done. Stuart and Binstead highlight the additional need to consider learning as social interaction.[9] This means that much learning is not independent from the organizational context in which the individual is placed. The organizational context can facilitate or inhibit the learner's ability to learn, and also the ability to learn how to learn.

For instance, individual learning within organizations can be facilitated if:

» learning is one of the key values of the organization;
» the CEO has a natural interest in learning;
» permission to think differently is given by the directors;
» defensiveness is generally discouraged;
» the organization does not suffer from a disproportionate sense of hierarchy; and
» errors are not seen as necessarily career-limiting.

However, individual learning within organizations can be inhibited if:

» performance is almost purely judged according to short-term internal measures and indicators;
» the organization is a "defender", with its main focus being to preserve rather than renew its position;
» top management are autocratic;

» top management espouse the need for openness and learning, but
  do not deal with difficult issues this way in practice; and
» there is excessive politicking.

Once learning is entangled in a more social organizational context,
the learning loops that are likely to occur (as per Kolb) are likely
to be much more difficult to complete. Thus, Kolb's learning theory
tends to focus primarily on *individual* rather than *group* learning.
Group learning involves not merely a learning stimulus but also a
learning vehicle of some kind. This learning vehicle may take the
form of a single meeting or a series of meetings. It may extend to a
substantive project, a workshop, or a wider and longer intervention in
an organization (as in the cases of Dowty Communications and Mercury
Communications described in Chapter 7).

Subsequent to experimentation, an important stage within the
learning process is filtering of the learning, as can be seen in Fig. 8.2.

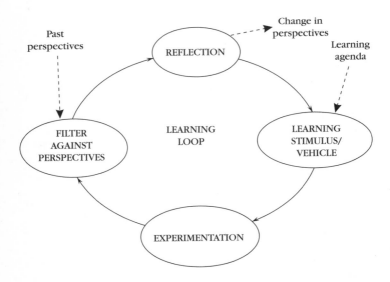

Fig. 8.2 Strategic learning – The learning loop.

Here, experiences are interpreted relative to past concepts, experiences, and feelings. Some of these may be peculiar to individuals, whereas others will be shared. Organizational theory is awash with terms for dealing with the filtering process, including *constructs*, *schema*, *frames of reference*, *mindsets*, and finally *perspectives* – the latter being the term that is perhaps closest to everyday speech.

Figure 8.3 develops the Kolb model by building in a second loop called the *action loop*, which begins by matching experiences to needs. This takes the learner back to the agendas that motivate action. Where individuals are learning as part of a group, their agendas will be multiple and overlapping, which explains why facilitation is of paramount importance not merely to move forward but to define the agendas.

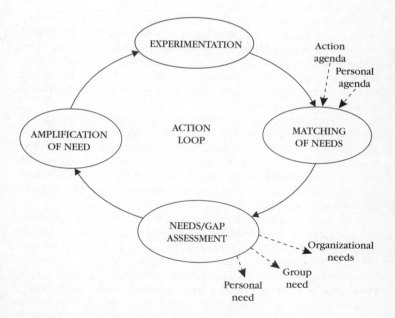

Fig. 8.3   Strategic learning – The action loop.

This is followed by an additional phase in the action loop – a more detailed needs assessment in order to identify areas for possible experimentation. At this stage, managers appear intuitively to relate needs to the perceived gap between where they are now and where they wish to be (or feel they ought to be).

A further important stage is that of amplifying the needs. This is important as experimentation will involve effort, and possibly some risk. It may also be in competition with other areas of opportunity for action. Often learning is viewed as an imperative by proponents of management learning – a good thing in itself, but in reality managers have so many competing claims on their time that rivalry for their attention is intense and acute. Therefore a critical success factor for more complex learning is that the perceived need to experiment increases. A second critical success factor is the ability to deal with distractions, which can be legion.

Figure 8.4 now integrates the learning and action loops so that we see complex learning as a dual system of action and learning. Within organizations both loops are in operation simultaneously, but are often not well synchronized. In some instances they may work against each other, for instance where learning insights occur but are not strong enough to challenge the major activities to which the organization is already deeply committed.

Important features in Fig. 8.4 are distraction and unlearning. Frequently, there may be such a degree of competition for managers' attention that instead of reinforcement (amplification of needs), the issues or insights are lost or lie unutilized as a result of distraction. This may be far from being the exception – much of the learning achieved in management workshops can be lost as the awareness of the problem rapidly folds back on itself once it has opened up.

It can be inferred that there is such a thing as a learning window of opportunity. Unless learning is capitalized on quickly, it rapidly becomes overlaid and may disintegrate owing to other issues and activities. This is not to say that it has ceased to exist.

Unlearning is another important process to be reckoned with. If new knowledge or skills are not used (and fairly soon), they rapidly decay. This is especially true when the learning is of a more complex and subtle

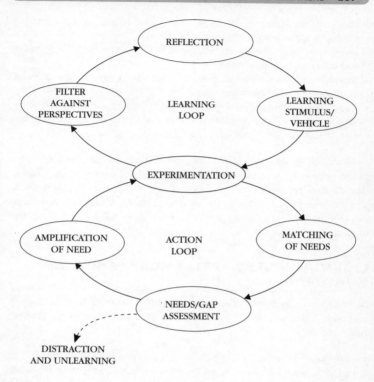

Fig. 8.4 Strategic learning – A dual system.

nature, as in the case of strategic learning. It is therefore important to amplify the needs and to have at least some early experimentation.

Finally, in the strategic learning process, it is possible to highlight a number of areas where the loops of learning can be facilitated, such as for:

» reflection – formal business analysis and evaluation frameworks for reflection and filtering;

» the learning stimulus – management workshops, projects, and reviews to act as learning stimuli and vehicles;
» experimentation – implementation frameworks for moving round or reducing barriers to change;
» matching of needs – measures and controls to assess how possible action is matched to needs; and
» needs/gap assessment – strategic positioning, or understanding where you are now against where you want to be, helps to assess needs and the gap between existing and desired states.

In addition, there may be powerful organizational "recipes" that guide decision-making in the organization. These recipes, or rules of thumb, may prescribe certain types of activity, or may prohibit them. These recipes can be shared by the organization or may be introduced by specific individuals, for instance by a new CEO hired from the outside.

LEARNING STYLES – PETER HONEY AND ALAN MUMFORD

Not all learners approach their learning with a single style. Peter Honey and Alan Mumford distinguish between four major styles of learning practiced by:

1 *activists*, who learn best when involved in concrete tasks;
2 *reflectors*, who learn best when reviewing and reflecting on what they have done and what has happened;
3 *theorists*, who learn best when they can relate information to concepts or change; and
4 *pragmatists*, who learn best when they can see the relevance of knowledge to real-life issues and problems.

Of course, none of these styles need be mutually exclusive. Honey and Mumford's approach is to say that for any individual, one style will tend to be predominant. This will affect the optimal choice of learning path for the individual. Anyone with a degree of training experience will say that groups as a whole are likely to have quite marked collective learning styles.

For example, in more cerebral industries, companies, or functions you might find that a particular group is quite quiet. This does not mean that they are not finding the learning useful. Often they are "soaking up" the learning. Although they may show less signs of outer activity and enthusiasm, they may be actually doing more learning than a set of bouncy activists.

*For example, take the following two learning groups encountered by one of the authors, in his capacity as tutor at the Cranfield School of Management, south central England. The first group was taking part in a public strategy program. The second group, consisting of staff from the Royal Bank of Scotland. was undertaking an in-company HR consulting program.

A TUTOR'S PERSPECTIVE
Learning group 1

My first impressions of this group were that they were very lively, with one or two highly participative, perhaps even dominant, individuals. When we began, they were late back from lunch and I could not get them to provide sufficient attention to get started. (I remember thinking, "Wow! I have not had this for five years! The last time was when I had that boisterous class of much younger MBA students.") As the afternoon progressed, I realized that besides being predominantly activist, the group contained a number of people who found it hard to take in much conceptual input.

The dynamics of the afternoon began to run more smoothly until one of the more dominant, hyperactive individuals (an all-out activist learner) suddenly said: "Sorry, but I just don't get it. I just don't get why writing a book called *Be Your Own Strategy Consultant* is such a cunning plan." (The purpose of this book, as I had already explained to them, was to redefine the rates of the strategic consulting industry and to position the students to help themselves.)

I tried three times to explain what I had meant, then elected to helicopter. But the damage was done – whilst about half of the participants got a lot out of the afternoon, a quarter got less and a quarter were negative. (This was a session I had delivered ten times previously, almost always with star ratings.)

This learning event was thus hindered by:

» a mismatch between my inputs (some conceptual and subtle) with the activist/pragmatist learning styles of the participants;
» personality issues amongst certain participants; and
» the participants not fully taking to my style.

Learning group 2

This was my eighth program with the Royal Bank of Scotland. All had gone well previously, and I had got used to a mix of participants who were primarily activists/pragmatists, with a sprinkling of reflectors/theorists. Normally this produced very lively sessions together, but for once this wasn't to happen.

The program director told me that the participants were "a bit quiet." "No kidding," I thought in the first input session. They were so quiet that it could have been another company I was working with.

But as the afternoon moved on and they listened intently to my inputs (as if in soak program), I realized that I had a bunch of reflectors/theorists. Their quietness actually signaled that they were in a highly focused learning mode. Although they were not visibly ecstatic at the end, the feedback was excellent, which was unexpected.

Before we leave Honey and Mumford, it is useful to flag up that they have developed a very useful learning styles questionnaire. Along with Belbin team role profiling and other personality tests, the questionnaire is a useful aid to managers wishing to acquire better knowledge of their own capability and potential. (See Chapter 9 for a fuller discussion of psychometric profiling tools.)

As most managers fall into the activist/pragmatist category, it is helpful not to overdose on conceptual input before getting them to perform a learning exercise. Once the activist/pragmatist has actually completed the learning task, they should then be able to do at least some reflection/abstract conceptualization (as per the Kolb learning cycle). However, they might well find it difficult to do so (as was the case with the first learning group) if they:

» are doing more complex, subtle learning;
» have mental maps that are relatively underdeveloped;
» entertain a relatively high opinion of their own intellectual capability; and
» want to make an impact on, or be liked by, the rest of the learning group.

ACTION LEARNING – REG REVANS AND MALCOLM KNOWLES

Reg Revans was perhaps the first to coin the term *action learning*. Meanwhile, Malcolm Knowles recognized that adults tend to learn in a different style to children. He therefore felt that management learning should be highly focused on actions that might lead directly to results of tangible value.

The key ingredients of action learning are:

» formal learning inputs, perhaps through a conventional short training event;
» work on group learning projects to deliver some beneficial decisions or actions; and
» mutual support within the learning group to self-manage the learning (such a group is known as a *learning set*).

The Mercury Communications case study in Chapter 7 is a classic example of an action learning program, although the learning groups were not explicitly called learning sets.

Action learning in its heyday was something of a fashion, which is a pity because most management learning can and should contain an action-targeted element. One of the key concepts within action learning is that of *self-directed learning*. In self-directed learning, the individual or group is the prime driver of the learning, and not the tutor. Unlike learning for children, where the main focus is often (but not always) the teacher, action learning is clear that the learner is king.

Action learning typically focuses on relatively high-reality learning and often involves some on-the-job element of experimentation.[10] Self-directed learning typically suits adults, who tend to prefer more concrete learning, as they can draw much more on their own past experience. They are also more likely to engage in learning if they see a potential pay-off in new knowledge, so helping them to perform more easily and effectively. As Knowles put it, "they do not learn for the sake of learning."

COMPLEX LEARNING – CHRIS ARGYRIS

Chris Argyris makes the distinction between *single-loop learning* (simple learning) and *double-loop learning* (more complex learning). Argyris's writings are sometimes a little hard to digest conceptually. However, the basic point he makes is that whilst single-loop learning concerns improving an existing competency, double-loop learning is often about developing a new competency or applying an existing competency to a new task. In double-loop learning the manager is thus reframing his mental maps, rather than simply infilling them or making marginal adjustments.

With double-loop learning there are obviously more possibilities for errors or mistakes. Rather than seeing these as positive learning experiences, most individuals will actually find their learning much inhibited by making errors.

To strengthen his argument, Argyris highlights an important dilemma – many managers and professionals are highly competent at doing the more routine and technical tasks, but they are often less competent at dealing with more open-ended, uncertain, and ambiguous issues. In particular, they may oversimplify problems. They may be very prone to oversimplification when alternative wider definitions of problems, either by others within the team or by outsiders, may imply error on their part.

This can lead to some rather blatantly defensive behaviors. Argyris calls these *self-sealing errors*. Paradoxically, clever individuals appear to be less inclined to admit to, let alone explore, errors. For instance, Argyris studied groups of strategy consultants and found that when a job went wrong, in their internal discussions they tended to push the responsibility back on to the client. They did not appear capable of reflecting on why errors had actually happened, not because they were stupid but because this was simply too uncomfortable, given their culture of being "clever."

The same phenomenon can be observed throughout managerial life. Errors often compound other errors, as management, rather than admit to mistakes, become more committed to their doomed causes. Sometimes an activity acquires its own momentum and appears unstoppable, for example when companies make a determined search for acquisitions. You then have a case of "rapidly escalating commitment."

So not only is it often difficult for individuals to reflect on what they have learned, but it is also difficult for groups to have a genuinely open learning style. Sometimes this can result in the dangerous condition known as *groupthink*, a concept that goes back to the US experience in Vietnam and also, vis-à-vis Cuba, in the Bay of Pigs debacle. Groupthink is the phenomenon where a group of individuals' perspectives on an issue converge so that they oversimplify reality and overlook uncertainties and risks.

Argyris graphically highlights the often chronic aversion to exposing error in his case studies. Let us now explore a more recent case at length to illustrate the differences between single-loop and double-loop learning.

SINGLE-LOOP AND DOUBLE-LOOP LEARNING – RAVEN INVESTMENTS

A dozen senior managers from a British financial services company, Raven Investments, were involved in a "strategy implementation" action learning program. The goals of this modular program were to:

» develop their capacity to think strategically;
» apply this capacity to how they manage operationally; and
» simulate both strategic thinking and action in two business development projects.

Before the program, the in-house resources manager applied psychometric tests to find out more about the mix of their management and learning styles. The results indicated that only a few of the managers had an innovative bent; most were highly action-oriented. They were, in the jargon of this particular test, out-and-out "thrusters."

The action learning program was structured in three phases.

1 A three-day workshop was conducted so that the managers could become acquainted with key strategic concepts and learn how to manage implementation strategically.
2 Data was collected for the business development project, back in the organization.
3 A five-day session was conducted off-site to analyze project data, and to create and evaluate options to be presented to board members.

Prior to the program, attempts were made by the facilitator to set expectations about the program's focus and style, but these were misinterpreted. As the facilitator arrived at the luxurious hotel in the Cotswolds, central England, and unloaded materials at the rear of the tropical swimming pool, he was being surreptitiously observed. Apparently, program members who thought they had been invited to a few days' course in pleasant circumstances became nervous at the scale of preparations. This looked like hard work and not the management holiday they had been expecting!

Despite a clear statement at the beginning of the program that it would involve a lot of lateral thinking, it was clear that the message had not been fully assimilated. By the second day, participants appeared to be getting jumpy and uncomfortable. One of the two learning groups had great trouble brainstorming ideas for the business development project, despite intensive facilitation.

Later that day, the facilitator decided that it was opportune to reflect on their learning experiences. He stated: "It seems that you have been struggling to move out of your normal way of thinking and learning. What we have been doing [writing on the flip chart] is dealing with a much messier pattern of ideas than your normal job accustoms you to. You need to be more patient in exploring the issues, while using the strategic tools and frameworks to give you focus and direction. Strategic thinking isn't about linear, deductive problem-solving; it is about fluid, creative thinking concerning issues where there are many uncertainties and where all our assumptions can be challenged.''

The managers visibly relaxed when the facilitator put it that way. This became a turning point for the program. Subsequently, both groups went on to produce projects that genuinely impressed Raven's board members by their depth of thinking and insight.

During the program, the individual styles of managers had made it difficult to jump-shift from single-loop to double-loop learning. At one stage one of the groups looked so depressed that, to lighten their mood, the facilitator suggested: ''Well, don't worry [turning to the window and opening it], I see we are on the second floor – who wants to jump out first?''

This joke broke the seriousness of the group. Double-loop learning doesn't have to be extremely serious or gloomy; on the contrary, it may need to be lightened up. Managers need to be in a relaxed state to be good at complex learning, not deeply worried about making mistakes and looking foolish. This incident highlights that not only is it difficult to shift gear into strategic double-loop learning, but it can also be worrying and potentially frightening for participants.

The key lessons from this case are as follows.

» If managers are deeply ingrained in their routine single-loop learning tracks, it is difficult to get them to jump on to more uncertain, complex, and possibly threatening learning tracks.
» Managers need to have a mix of support but firm guidance. (In this case, another breakthrough occurred when the facilitator appeared to lose patience and said, ''You really must let go of the old ways of looking at things.'' This helped the managers to see the facilitator as ''one of them'' and not just another ''human resources type.'')
» If there are a number of tools and frameworks with which managers are unfamiliar, or the focus of learning is beyond their more recent experience, they need considerably more time to gain a sound learning platform – and confidence.

» Sometimes it may be wise to give participants control over the issue of presenting outputs to senior management. If participants feel in control of when and whether to present outputs, and indeed of what to present, they will tend to experience less uncertainty and fear.
» Although double-loop learning is difficult (and more so for some than for others), it is possible to orchestrate it with managers working in learning groups. The problem, however, is how to *sustain* the learning once the learning group is disbanded.

The above case highlights how difficult it may be in some organizations to become more fluid or to introduce more open systems of learning. Even when a learning setting is created deliberately, there are many forces inhibiting learning, including barriers and anxieties. One way to alleviate these problems is to expose individuals to *systems thinking*.

SYSTEMS THINKING AND SCENARIOS – PETER SENGE

Systems thinking is the idea that an organization (or an individual) operates as an organic system, in which one variable impacts on another and ultimately loops back on itself, bringing helpful learning feedback. Peter Senge's main contribution to systems thinking was to highlight the need to think about problems and issues in such a way as to capture their key interdependencies. We have already considered fishbone analysis (see Chapter 4) as a way of solving problems, but quite often the root causes of problems are interdependent and need exploring (BP's Project 1990, outlined in Chapter 5, marked an exploratory attempt of this kind).

Using such systems thinking, it is much easier to:

» visualize a problem and see the bigger picture;
» scope and evaluate possible strategies to intervene in the problem; and

» communicate the complex nature of the problem within the organization.

Let us now look at systems thinking in terms of *scenarios*.

Scenarios

Scenarios are projected chains of events that constitute a vehicle for learning, whether at corporate, business, departmental, team, or individual level. Scenarios are not static and comprehensive views of the future. Scenarios are in many ways more like a video film – they are of necessity selective but contain a dynamic storyline. Scenarios thus contain a series of images, rather than a single image, of the future. The images hang together by means of the storyline.

Again like a video film, the story can be run forward or (alternatively) backward. By replaying the story, you can work backwards from a particular scenario to see what events might bring about a particular outcome. (These events have been described as "transitional events."[11])

Scenarios are therefore not an excuse for making broad or vague generalizations; as they consist of images, they have a clarity about them that enables recognition. Managers need to know which world they are entering into, so the resolution must be sharp not fuzzy. In the words of Ansoff, scenarios provide ways of picking up, amplifying, and interpreting weak signals in your environment.[12] Scenarios are not:

» mere forecasts;
» projections from past trends;
» fixed or rigid world views;
» complete in all details; and
» static.

Scenario analysis is particularly useful for developing the individual, from three important perspectives.

1 Scenarios can be used to improve an individual's imagination and their ability to anticipate the future, both of which can lead to a higher degree of proactivity.

2 They can be used to improve everyday management capability.
3 They can be of great help in developing career strategy.

For example, scenarios to stretch your longer-term imagination might cover:

» market and competitive change;
» the impact of an economic slowdown;
» the impact of a major disruptive event (like September 11);
» new technology; and
» organizational change.

These areas are covered in strategy books such as *Exploring Corporate Strategy* by Johnson and Scholes,[13] so I will not dwell on them here.

This is not to underestimate the importance of longer-term scenarios; they are likely to play a big impact on your career prospects, whether in your existing organization or in a new one. But scenarios can have greater impact and more frequent use at an everyday level, for instance in:

» specific projects;
» on-the-job relationships;
» meetings;
» workshops; and
» personal development.

Career development scenarios are extremely helpful for most managers. In the exercise that follows, try and answer the questions for one possible future job. (See also Chapter 6 for related exercises.)

EXERCISE – CAREER SCENARIOS (15 MINS)

1 How might the external context of the job (department, company, industry) change over the period of doing it?
2 How well would your boss support you? Might your boss change jobs?
3 How well would you perform the job? If poorly, then what might cause this?

4 What new career opportunities might be opened up for you as a result of doing this job?

5 What career opportunities might be closed down for you?

6 How might your feelings about the job change over time, and how might these influence your performance and next career move?

7 What other job opportunities might occur in the course of this particular job, and how might you respond to them?

NEUROLINGUISTIC PROGRAMMING – JOHN GRINDER AND RICHARD BANDLER

Neurolinguistic programming (NLP) can be a further way for an individual to find a development path. But what actually is *neurolinguistic programming*? The term can be broken down into the following three elements.

1 *Neuro* refers to our thinking or perception, as determined by the activity of the brain or nervous system. Specifically, it refers to the neurological processes of sensing, namely seeing, hearing, feeling, tasting, and smelling.

2 *Linguistic* refers to the language patterns that affect our understanding and form the basis of much communication. It is hard to imagine conscious thought without language – how often do we have conversations with ourselves, give ourselves advice, tell off the telly?

3 *Programming* refers to the way that we organize our thoughts, feelings, and beliefs so as to bring about desired changes in behavior and outcome (much as we program a computer for specific tasks with appropriate software).

The origins of NLP lie in both linguistics and psychology. NLP was started in the 1970s by John Grinder, a teacher of linguistics, and Richard Bandler, a researcher in psychology with an interest in linguistics. Grinder and Bandler modeled how three internationally acclaimed psychotherapists went about their work. They derived certain best-practice behavioral models from their observations, in order to pass these "recipes" on to other people in the field.

NLP brings together a plethora of approaches from a multitude of sources. The particular integration of learning systems does add value to the individual parts, which are valuable in themselves. Some of these concepts go back to very basic psychology. The founding principles of NLP are as follows.

» *Decide what you want* – setting goals is a precondition of successful achievement.
» *Do something* – without a need to act, problems will not be addressed and opportunities will not be taken up.
» *Notice what happens* – how do we sense what is going on? This depends on our powers of observation, which may vary in their focus depending on our sensory preferences.
» *Be flexible* – the person who has maximum flexibility in their behavior controls the system of which they form a part.

In NLP there is also a good deal of emphasis on *how* one communicates, with the various modes being classified as usual, auditory, and kinesthetic. NLP suggests that each and every person, in their use of words, exhibits preferences in how they communicate. According to NLP, if two people have wildly opposing preferences, they will almost inevitably have problems and tensions in their relationship. NLP makes one more aware of one's communication style preferences.

Goal-setting is another focus of NLP. One approach is to map out a personal hierarchy of goals, which get more and more specific. Figure 8.5 shows how this might be done, beginning with a meta-goal like happiness, which cascades down to more specific areas like work and wealth.

NLP furnishes some potentially useful constructs or categories that can be applied to the interpretation of our own behavior and that of others, making their meaning more understandable. Unfortunately, it has also produced a battery of linguistic jargon, including:

» *complex equivalence* – two statements that are meant to mean the same thing (e.g. "she walked past me" and "she is annoyed");
» *content reframing* – focusing on another part or aspect of a statement or experience to give it a different meaning;

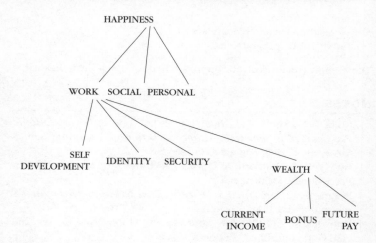

Fig. 8.5 NLP and goals.

» *dissociated* – seeing an experience as if through someone else's eyes or from outside yourself; and
» *meta-model* – a model that identifies imprecise language patterns, and gives questions and responses to clarify or challenge them.

In short, the value of NLP is that it provides a collection of practical techniques and thought processes for helping the individual to become *more aware* of their psychological make-up, and how it influences their behavior and interactions with other people. In learning and development terms, NLP is excellent at recognizing how the personality needs to be managed in order to secure a more effective development path.

SUMMARY

There are many key developmental concepts, including:

» learning as feedback;
» learning styles;
» action learning;

» complex learning;
» systems thinking and scenarios; and
» neurolinguistic programming.

These imply a highly eclectic approach to developing the individual.

NOTES

1 Kolb, D.A., Rubin, I.M., & McIntyre, J.M. (1971) *Organizational Psychology: An experiential approach to organizational behavior*. Prentice Hall, Englewood Cliffs, NJ.

2 Honey, P. & Mumford, A. (1982) *The Manual of Learning Styles*. Peter Honey, Maidenhead.

3 Revans, R.W. (1980) *Action Learning: New techniques for management*. Blond & Briggs, London.

4 Knowles, M.S. (1978) *The Adult Learner: A neglected species*, 2nd edn. Gulf Publishing, London & Houston.

5 Argyris, C. (1991) "Teaching smart people how to learn," *Harvard Business Review*, May–June.

6 Senge, P. (1990) *The Fifth Discipline: The art and practice of the learning organization*. Doubleday, New York.

7 Grinder, J. & Bandler, R. (1994) *NLP: The new art and science of getting what you want*. Piatkus Books, London.

8 Honey & Mumford, op.cit.

9 Stuart, R. & Binstead, D. (1981) "The transfer of learning I and II," *New Approaches to Management Development* (ed. B. Nixon), pp. 71–108. Gower, Aldershot.

10 Ibid.

11 Grundy, A.N. & Brown, L. (2002) *Be Your Own Strategy Consultant: Demystifying strategic thinking*. Thomson Learning, London.

12 Ansoff, H.I. (1975) "Managing strategic surprise by response to weak signals," *Californian Management Review*, xviii, winter, pp. 21–3.

13 Johnson, G. & Scholes, K. (1989) *Exploring Corporate Strategy*. Prentice Hall, Hemel Hempstead.

Resources

» Psychometric profiling tools
» Belbin team roles
» Useful books

The main resources in this chapter are psychometric profiling tools, such as the Belbin team role model. First, we take a cursory look at these tools in general, before focusing on Belbin team roles. We then list some useful books that you might wish to read as part of your individual development.

PSYCHOMETRIC PROFILING TOOLS

Good tests for a psychometric profiling tool are as follows.

1 It should be a *sensitive* measuring instrument, which discriminates well between subjects.
2 It should have been *standardized* on a representative and sizeable sample of the target population, so that any individual's score can be interpreted in relation to others.
3 It should be *reliable* in the sense of always measuring the same thing. A test aimed at measuring a particular characteristic should measure the same characteristic when applied to different people at the same time, or to the same person at different times.
4 It should be *valid* in the sense of measuring the characteristic that it is intended to measure. Thus, an intelligence test should measure intelligence and not simply verbal ability.[1]

A psychometric profiling tool is only one of many inputs that can help an individual to chart a development path. These other important inputs include:

» data on past on-the-job performance;
» 360-degree feedback (from boss, peers, and subordinates);
» discussion with your boss;
» discussion with a coach or mentor;
» informal feedback from your peers and subordinates; and
» discussion with your friends or partner (what do they say you would be naturally good at, or not?).

Psychometric profiling tools can be used for a variety of purposes such as:

» recruitment procedures; and
» assessment procedures (e.g. selecting potential candidates for more senior jobs).

They can serve both the individual and the organization in different ways, as we shall see with Belbin team roles. Other psychometric profiling tools include:

» intelligence/IQ tests, which typically focus on visual and verbal reasoning, and numeracy skills;
» analytical tests, such as the graduate management admission test (GMAT) used to select candidates for MBA programs; and
» personality tests, notably the sixteen personality factor (16PF) questionnaire and the occupational personality questionnaire (OPQ).

BELBIN TEAM ROLES

Belbin team roles deal with how individuals can work more effectively as team players. They can be used by a team to:

» help individuals identify their professed team role styles and so develop their personal effectiveness;
» encourage specific individuals to try out and develop their skills in other team role styles;
» diagnose the overall strengths and weaknesses of the team as a whole;
» help manage team dynamics more effectively; and
» help plan future moves into and out of the team, so aiding team formation.

Invariably, the use of Belbin team roles sparks a shift in self-awareness, and thus in effectiveness, within the team. It was certainly found to be essential by Mercury Communications (see case study in Chapter 7).

The key Belbin team roles are as follows:

» plant
» shaper
» implementer
» coordinator
» monitor evaluator
» completer finisher
» teamworker
» resource investigator.

Plant

Plants are innovators and can be highly creative, providing ideas for major developments. They may prefer to work by themselves at some distance from the team, using their imagination and often working in an innovative way. They may tend to be introverted, and are inclined to react to criticism and to praise. Their ideas may often be off the wall, and need shaping.

The main use of a plant is to generate new proposals and solve complex problems. Plants are often needed in the initial stages of a project or when a project is failing to progress. Plants have usually made their mark as founders of companies or as originators of new products.

The plant was so named when it was found that one of the best ways to improve the performance of an ineffective and uninspired team was to "plant" such a team type in it. But you can also think of the plant as the team member who provides the basic ideas for growth.

The tendency with the plant is that they will devote too much creative energy to ideas that may appeal to them but do not contribute to the team's strategic and personal objectives. They may be put off if their ideas are rejected and may even withdraw from the team, at least temporarily. It can take quite a lot of careful handling and judicious flattery (usually by the coordinator) to get the best out of the plant. But for all their faults, it is the plant that provides the vital spark.

Too many plants in one team, however, may be counterproductive as they tend to spend their time reinforcing their own ideas and engaging each other in combat.

Shaper

Shapers are highly motivated with lots of energy. Usually they are extroverts and possess strong drive. Shapers encourage others to do things. In the face of barriers, they will find a way round. Shapers are excellent at putting energy into a team and are useful in groups where politics would otherwise dominate. They are well suited to making necessary changes and do not mind taking less popular viewpoints. They will always try to impose some shape on the group discussion.

The shaper sees the team as an extension of their ego. They want action and they want it immediately. There is a danger that people inside the team are likely to be steamrollered by the shaper.

Implementer

Implementers have a lot of common sense and self-control. They love hard work and like to tackle problems systematically. They are usually less concerned with the pursuit of self-interest. Implementers may lack spontaneity and not easily be able to change direction.

They are useful to an organization because of their capacity for work and because of their consistency. They succeed because they are efficient and because they have a sense of what is directly relevant and practicable. An implementer will do what needs to be done.

Coordinator

Coordinators are able to help others to work towards shared goals. Mature and confident, they are very good at delegating and channeling activities in the pursuit of group objectives.

Coordinators are particularly useful when running a team with diverse skills and personal characteristics. Coordinators may well conflict with shapers due to their contrasting styles.

The coordinator sees most clearly which member of the team is strong or weak in each area of the team's function, and focuses people on what they do best. They are conscious of the need to use the team's combined resources as effectively as possible. The coordinator is the one who defines roles and work boundaries, identifying any gaps and filling them.

Monitor evaluator

Monitor evaluators are very sensible team members, who do not get carried away by impractical ideas. They are slow decision-makers and prefer to think things over. Monitor evaluators have well-developed judgment and highly critical thinking ability.

Although by nature a critic rather than a creator, the monitor evaluator does not usually criticize just for the sake of it but only if they can see a flaw in a project. The monitor evaluator is often the least highly motivated of the team; enthusiasm and euphoria are simply not part of their agenda. This shortcoming is redeemed by their detachment and objectivity. The monitor evaluator is excellent at assimilating, interpreting, and evaluating large volumes of complex data; analyzing problems; and assessing the judgments and contributions of others.

Completer finisher

Completer finishers have a huge capacity for follow-through and attention to detail. They will not start anything that they cannot finish. They tend to be anxious inside, yet externally they may appear relaxed. They are typically introverted and are often not keen on delegating.

Completer finishers are invaluable where the project requires close concentration to detail. They bring a sense of urgency to the team and are good at meeting deadlines. The completer finisher tends not to be an assertive member of the team but generates an ongoing sense of low-key urgency, which keeps the team moving forward towards its goals.

Teamworker

Teamworkers help to support the team's morale. They are particularly concerned about other members of the team; they are adaptable to different situations and people, and are always diplomatic. They tend to be popular members of a group.

Teamworkers help to prevent interpersonal disruption within the group, and thus allow all team members to contribute effectively. They will go to great lengths to avoid interpersonal clashes. As a promoter of team harmony, the teamworker counterbalances the tensions that can be caused by the shaper and the plant.

Resource investigator

Resource investigators are often enthusiastic extroverts. They are good at networking with people both inside and outside the team. They are adept at exploring new opportunities and developing contacts. They are particularly good at picking up other people's ideas and developing them. They are also skilled at finding out what is available and what can be done.

EXERCISE – WHICH BELBIN TEAM ROLE CORRESPONDS TO YOUR OWN? (10 MINS)

1 For each team role typology – plant, shaper, implementer, coordinator, monitor evaluator, completer finisher, teamworker, and resource investigator – rate yourself on a scale of 1 to 5 (in which 1 = hardly applies at all, 2 = applies a little, 3 = applicable, 4 = very applicable, 5 = extremely applicable).

2 Extract the "So what?" from this profiling by asking yourself:
   i) Which are your two most-favored role styles, and what significance does this have?
   ii) Which are your two least-favored role styles, and what significance does this have?
   iii) What effect does this profiling have on how you operate in your current team?

Impact on group work

It is useful to examine how Belbin team roles impact on group work as follows.

» The plant generates off-the-wall ideas, which feed into breakthrough thinking. But, on their own, these ideas may be half-formed and underdeveloped, and may fail in practice.
» The shaper helps to develop strategic ideas into workable strategies.
» The implementer actually helps get the implementation done.
» The coordinator brings together the ideas of different team members, and reconciles them. The coordinator also establishes the key roles, so people know what they are doing.
» The monitor evaluator helps to make the ideas into an effective business case, and monitors results.
» The completer finisher maintains a focus on project milestones.
» The teamworker harmonizes team interaction and personal agendas.
» The resource investigator ensures that interfaces with the organizational environment happen smoothly.

Managing your preferred team roles explicitly is an essential part of the development of any individual. But you also need to be aware of other aspects of your psychological make-up.

Link

www.belbin.com

USEFUL BOOKS

The following is a list of useful books for self-managed learning. Not only will these open up a whole variety of new management perspectives, but they will also give you an excellent taster of the essence of an MBA. Here are three handy hints for readers.

1 *Try to complete one chapter per week.* Consider booking some work time (say an hour a week) in which to do this.
2 *Draw out the specific learning lessons and action points for each book.* How has the book made you think or feel differently? What will you now stop doing, do differently, or do entirely anew?
3 *Remember that you don't need to read everything.* Practice the art of speed-reading, and try to focus on the 20% of things that will add 80% of the value.

Strategy

Grundy, A.N. & Brown, L. (2002) *Be Your Own Strategy Consultant: Demystifying strategic thinking.* Thomson Learning, London. (A comprehensive and illustrated guide to the practice of strategy.)

Hamel, G. & Prahalad, C.K. (1994) *Competing for the Future.* Harvard Business School Press, Boston. (A blueprint for how an organization can create future markets.)

Mintzberg, H. (1994) *The Rise and Fall of Strategic Planning.* Financial Times Prentice Hall, London & New York. (A critique of conventional planning processes.)

Mintzberg, H., Ahlstrand, B., & Lampel, J. (1998) *Strategy Safari: A guided tour through the wilds of strategic management.* Prentice Hall, London. (A multi-perspective account of the different schools of strategy.)

Finance

Ellis, J. & Williams, D. (1993) *Corporate Strategy and Financial Analysis: Managerial, accounting and stock market perspectives*. Pitman Publishing, London. (An incisive account of strategic insights from financial reporting.)

Grundy, A.N. (2001) *Shareholder Value*. Capstone, Oxford. (Demystifies shareholder value theory and shows how economic value links to strategy and organizational mindsets.)

Kaplan, R.S. & Norton, D.P. (1990) *The Balanced Scorecard: Translating strategy into action*. Harvard Business School Press, Boston. (The seminal work on the balanced scorecard for corporate control.)

McTaggart, J.M., Kontes, P.W., & Mankins, M.C. (1994) *The Value Imperative: Managing for superior shareholder returns*. Free Press, London & New York. (An everyday account of managing for shareholder value.)

Ward, K. (1993) *Corporate Financial Strategy*. Butterworth-Heinemann, Oxford. (A reasonably untechnical overview of corporate finance.)

Acquisitions and alliances

Brady, C. & Lorenz, A. (2001) *End of the Road: BMW and Rover: A brand too far*. Financial Times Prentice Hall, London. (A graphic account of the perils of mismanaged acquisitions.)

Brummer, A. & Cowe, R. (1994) *Hanson: A biography*. Fourth Estate, London. (Fascinating insights into the rise of Hanson plc and its approach to acquisitions.)

Doz, Y.L. & Hamel, G. (1998) *The Alliance Advantage*. Harvard Business School Press, Boston. (A good account of the pathways and pitfalls of alliances.)

Faulkner, D. (1995) *International Strategic Alliances: Co-operating to compete*. McGraw-Hill, London & New York. (A thoughtful view of the evolutionary dynamics of alliances over time, and how to manage them.)

Haspeslagh, P.C. & Jemison, D.B. (1991) *Managing Acquisitions: Creating value through corporate renewal*. Free Press, London & New York. (The seminal and exhaustive work on the stage-by-stage process of acquisitions.)

Lorange, P. & Roos, J. (1992) *Strategic Alliances: Formation, implementation, and evolution*. Blackwell Business, Oxford. (The European alliance gurus give an excellent account of alliance strategy.)

Marketing

Doyle, P. (1994) *Marketing Management and Strategy*. Prentice Hall, London & New York. (An excellent book on the strategic aspects of marketing.)

Kotler, P. (2000) *Marketing Management*, 10th edn. Prentice Hall International, London. (The classic textbook on marketing.)

Creativity and innovation

Dyson, J. (1997) *Against the Odds: An autobiography*. Orion Publishing, London. (How Dyson wrestled UK market leadership from Hoover through product/market innovation.)

Turner, S. (2002) *Tools for Success*. McGraw-Hill, London. (A good guide to a variety of techniques for solving management problems.)

Operations

Andersen, E.S., Grude, K.V., Haug, T., & Gibbons, T. (1987) *Goal Directed Project Management*. Kogan Page, London. (A thorough workbook on the project management process.)

Evans, P. & Wurster, T.S. (2000) *Blown to Bits: How the new economics of information transforms strategy*. Harvard Business School Press, Boston. (The role of the Internet in operations strategy.)

Grundy, A.N. & Brown, L.B. (2002) *Strategic Project Management: Creating organizational breakthroughs*. Thomson Learning, London. (How strategic projects can be managed.)

Hammer, M. & Champy, J. (1993) *Re-engineering the Corporation: A manifesto for business revolution*. Nicholas Brealey Publishing, London. (The textbook on business process re-engineering.)

Organization

Holbeche, L. (1999) *Aligning Human Resources and Business Strategy*. Butterworth-Heinemann, Oxford. (Developing HR strategy.)

Ulrich, D. & Lake, D. (1999) *Organizational Capability: Competing from the inside out*. Wiley & Sons, New York. (An alternative view of competitive advantage using internal competencies to deliver superior value.)

Leadership and personal skills

Adair, J. (1986) *Effective Teambuilding*. Gower, Aldershot. (A simple account of team-building.)

Downey, M. (1999) *Effective Coaching*. Orion Business Books, London. (A practical guide on how to coach.)

Hooper, A. & Potter, J. (1997) *The Business of Leadership: Adding lasting value to your organization*. Ashgate Publications, Aldershot. (A useful overview of leadership.)

NOTES

1 Armstrong, M. (1991) *A Handbook of Personal Management Practice*. Kogan Page, London.

Ten Steps to Making

it Work

1 Diagnose the present
2 Image the future and create a stretching vision
3 Prioritize competency gaps
4 Focus on a small number of breakthroughs
5 Target the value added
6 Manage the interdependencies
7 Invest in sufficient consolidation
8 Get two for the price of one
9 Think laterally about the options
10 Development is ongoing and forever

INTRODUCTION

In this very short chapter, we give you ten quick high-level pointers on how value can be added by individual development.

1. DIAGNOSE THE PRESENT

Before looking at training solutions, you first need to understand what competencies exist or add value, and identify where and why there are gaps (e.g. by using fishbone analysis – see Chapter 4).

2. IMAGE THE FUTURE AND CREATE A STRETCHING VISION

But more important, in many ways, is the need to think about where you as an individual (and your organization too) might be in the future. This involves imaging the future – in perhaps two, three, five, or even ten years' time – and doing some stretch-thinking on what might actually be possible.

3. PRIORITIZE COMPETENCY GAPS

Each competency gap should be appraised in terms of how weak one is at the specific competency and how important the competency actually is, both now and in the future.

4. FOCUS ON A SMALL NUMBER OF BREAKTHROUGHS

Once you have reached this stage, it is crucial to segregate competencies for development into breakthroughs (no more than three at any specific time) and those for development into continuous improvements.

5. TARGET THE VALUE ADDED

This book highlights that it is actually possible to put a targeted financial value, albeit indicative, on what the benefits of individual development might be.

6. MANAGE THE INTERDEPENDENCIES

Training and development do not add value in isolation, but require alignment with performance management, career development, and on-the-job activities and challenges.

7. INVEST IN SUFFICIENT CONSOLIDATION

Much learning and development is wasted because of learning decay resulting from a lapse of time or a lack of practice. Courses, in particular, are inefficient vehicles of development unless follow-up activity is planned and actually performed.

8. GET TWO FOR THE PRICE OF ONE

Try to get both learning and business benefits simultaneously. This not only yields indirect spin-offs but also reinforces the learning.

9. THINK LATERALLY ABOUT THE OPTIONS

Training and development can be accomplished by a considerable range of options. Often options are selected by default, and this is unlikely to be particularly efficient or effective.

10. DEVELOPMENT IS ONGOING AND FOREVER

Development is absolutely not something to do just at the early to middle stages of your career. It needs to go on forever, otherwise you might as well begin your retirement plans in earnest!

CONCLUSION

With these ten steps in mind, we hope you can grasp that every second in management is a *learning moment*, and not just a *doing moment*.

This book should have given you a new range of insights into your own individual development. Do begin to put these into practice. For, if you don't, you may well share the fate of the turkeys in this fable:

"Once upon a time, an enterprising turkey gathered the flock together and, with demonstrations and instructions, taught them how to fly. All afternoon they enjoyed soaring, glimpsing new vistas.

"After the training was over, all the turkeys walked home."

Moral

Don't slip back out of individual development into turkey management.

Frequently Asked Questions (FAQs)

Q1: How is the nature of individual development changing, and why?

A: See Chapters 3 and 8.

Q2: What are the options for individual development, and how do they compare?

A: See Chapters 1 and 3.

Q3: What are the key concepts in individual development, and what do they mean?

A: See Chapters 2 and 8.

Q4: What is the return on individual development training?

A: See Chapters 3 and 7.

Q5: What does individual development mean in a global context?

A: See Chapter 5.

Q6: How do you define what business you are in?

A: See Chapter 6.

Q7: What are your key sources of personal competitive advantage, and how can you develop these?

A: See Chapter 6.

Q8: How might you formulate and evaluate a strategy for your career?

A: See Chapter 6.

Q9: How would you stage a learning intervention to develop a group of individuals?

A: See Chapter 7.

Q10: How do individuals learn most effectively, and what are the different forms of learning?

A: See Chapters 1, 3, and 8.

Index

EXPRESSEXEC –
BUSINESS THINKING AT YOUR FINGERTIPS

ExpressExec is a 12-module resource with 10 titles in each module. Combined they form a complete resource of current business practice. Each title enables the reader to quickly understand the key concepts and models driving management thinking today.

Available from:
www.expressexec.com

Customer Service Department
John Wiley & Sons Ltd
Southern Cross Trading Estate
1 Oldlands Way, Bognor Regis
West Sussex, PO22 9SA
Tel: +44(0)1243 843 294
Fax: +44(0)1243 843 303
Email: cs-books@wiley.co.uk